Great Battles of Biblical History

Also by Sir Richard Gale

WITH THE SIXTH AIRBORNE DIVISION IN NORMANDY
CALL TO ARMS

Masada

GENERAL SIR RICHARD GALE

Great Battles
of Biblical History
10122

 HUTCHINSON OF LONDON

HUTCHINSON & CO (*Publishers*) LTD
178-202 Great Portland Street
London W1

London   Melbourne   Sydney
Auckland   Bombay   Toronto
Johannesburg   New York

First published 1968

This book has been set in Plantin
by The Garden City Press Limited
Letchworth, Hertfordshire

09 089620 3

Many of the place names used in the Old Testament and in biblical times are not to be found in the modern atlas; in many cases their accurate situation is uncertain and in some unknown. An attempt to identify accurately all places mentioned has proved a baffling task. I have, therefore, included at the end of this book a glossary and gazetteer which I hope will be of use in fixing locations as well as indicating the meaning and significance of names where these might be of interest.

All dates that are mentioned in text are B.C.

Contents

Illustrations

Preface

The idea of writing this book commenced when, on reading the life of Lord Allenby, I found he had frequently consulted the Old Testament in considering the battles that lay ahead. When, much later, I myself served in Palestine my dormant interests were revived. I learned to love the land as I walked over the battlefields of biblical times. It was stimulating to stand at places like Megiddo; to gaze over the Vale of Esdraelon and look down on the River Kishon; to walk over the slopes of Mount Tabor and to recall Deborah's defeat of Sisera; to climb Gilboa where Saul faced the Philistines; to approach the Hills of Samaria and the road to Jerusalem via the Shechem of old; and to roam over the countryside of Galilee and up the valleys that led through the Shephelah to the mountains of Judaea. Except that the country is today well supplied with roads it must have looked, as I saw it, much as it did when the campaigns and battles of biblical history were fought.

When, in 1958, I was asked to write on the subject for the *Evening Standard* I readily accepted. I am grateful to the Editor for his permission to make use of this material.

How near historical fact can the events and even the individuals claim to be? Some of the tales are so old that they inevitably contain much that is legend, and the line between legend and fact can, indeed, at times be blurred.

Where I believe fact and legend to be in conflict I have

commented on this, and when legendary happenings seem to be opposed by reason I have put in my own interpretation of what occurred. However, the uncertain line dividing legend from history is not peculiar to biblical times, for in our own country we are faced by the romance that attaches to King Arthur. Of this tangled web the ancien poet Wace wrote: 'Nor all a lie, nor all true, nor all fable, nor all known, so much have the story-tellers told and the fablers fabled in order to embellish their tales, that they have made all seem false.'

Nevertheless, it is remarkable the extent to which the evidence of stone inscriptions, papyrus writings, the discoveries of the archaeologists and the known facts concerning the larger civilizations that surrounded Canaan corroborate these stories. For my facts and for my point of departure I have taken the text of the Old Testament, and I have consulted histories and the writings of numerous authorities, the more important of which I have tabulated.

One might wonder whether there are any lessons that could possibly apply to the world in which we live today. Have conditions so changed that there is nothing we can glean save knowledge of fact from these stories? The more I have gone into the battles and the more I have studied the characters of the principal actors, the more convinced have I become that the basic problems thay had to face and the principles of war that they applied have a validity today. Thus, in addition to their inherent interest, they do contain lessons for us and this, perhaps, is the principal justification for this book.

1 The strategic significance of the biblical lands

This book is concerned with events and the great men who shaped them in that part of the Near East generally known as the Fertile Crescent. It is an area that has had and still has considerable strategic significance. The term is appropriately used to describe the vast fruitful zone which, springing from the Persian Gulf, runs up the Tigris and Euphrates valleys to Damascus then, bending southwards, follows the Levant before finally disappearing in the Negeb and the deserts beyond. We are primarily concerned with that part which in more recent times has familiarly been known as Palestine.

In the most distant past this land, then ill-defined geographically, was called Matu. The first Sargon, who founded the ancient Akkadian Empire in Babylonia, referred to it as the Land of the Amorites, but the area he was considering included most of Syria. The ancient Arabs called it Esh-Sham, meaning The Left; just as they called Southern Arabia El Yemen, meaning The Right. The Greeks referred to it generally as Syria, but they included all the land from the Caucasus to the Mediterranean. Later it went by the name Phoenicia, a name derived from the Phoenicians who were a branch of the Semitic peoples occupying the coast above Mount Carmel. The name Palestine, which came from the Philistines, was used until 1948. The Turks referred to it as the Sanjak of Jerusalem and the Vilayet of Beyrut. In biblical times it was known as

Canaan. Canaan is, therefore, the term I shall use in this narrative.

Now Canaan, in contrast to the desert lands around was a 'land flowing with milk and honey.' To what did it owe its fertility? perhaps it was to Mount Hermon. This massive mountain, rising to over nine thousand feet above sea level, is on its upper slopes almost always covered with snow. To the west of Mount Hermon, not fifteen miles distant, Mount Lebanon rises majestically from the sea, but is some three thousand feet lower than her sister. The massif of which these two peaks are the southern crowns forms the watershed of four important rivers. The Orontes, which flows northwards, empties itself into the Mediterranean; the Arbana rushes eastwards eventually meandering across the plains around Damascus where it disappears into the sand; the Litany or Leontes flows south for a while through beautiful gorges before turning westwards to the Mediterranean; and finally the River Jordan which flows south until it drops into the Dead Sea.

If one stands on the Hills of Galilee the eye is naturally drawn to the massive white-capped gleaming slopes of Mount Hermon. From her and from her sister spring the fresh and bubbling waters of the Upper Jordan. Stretching south like two great fingers run the mountains that form the watershed of the Jordan; those to the east are called the Heights of Bashan, Gilead, Ammon and Moab; while those to the west are known as the Hills of Galilee, Samaria and Judea and constitute the great central range of Canaan.

The Jordan is more than a river-bed, it is a rift that, after passing through the Dead Sea, emerges again as the bed of the Red Sea. For the most part it is below sea level and where it enters the Dead Sea it passes through the lowest piece of land in the world. It divides the area into two distinct parts separating the fertile land of Canaan from the arid deserts to the east. The crossings over the river are few and are consequently of considerable military importance.

The hills of Canaan throw off spurs which gently fall into the coastal plain. The exceptions are the massif of the Lebanon and

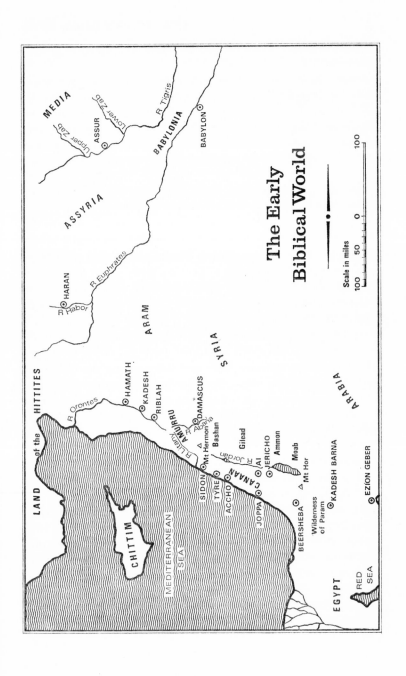

The Early
Biblical World

Mount Carmel which both drop precipitously to the sea and are consequently of strategic significance. From the hills of Canaan can be seen the deep blue of the Mediterranean and the pleasant coastal lands which, after rain, are green and beautiful to behold. The whole mountain system, though rugged in places, is in the north covered with forests of tall cedars that give wealth in the timber they yield and coolness in the shade they provide. On the lower slopes and in the green valleys are groves of olive trees and vineyards, while the streams that run down their sides provide water for man and beast. On the mountains themselves there is endless grazing for flocks.

Canaan is a small country. From the slopes of Mount Hermon to the barren wastes of the Negeb is only one hundred and fifty miles and the greatest breadth of the land is seventy. Such a country could not hold a population of sufficient size to defy either the might of Egypt on the one hand or that of the Euphrates and Tigris kingdoms on the other; but united and judiciously led it held a strategic position of obvious political and military importance. We shall see that, when united, its position gave both power and prestige to its people; we shall also see how, when internal dissension and petty jealousies banished patriotism and reason, this position was inevitably lost.

What of the countries bordering Canaan? To the east and the south lay the deserts of Arabia, windswept areas of sand and rock. Here, for the most part, there was neither water nor rainfall; there was only dew. Yet, always when the dew fell in the cool night, some little green would grow and, as though to defy nature, the flowering crocus would break through the crevices where rock and sand met. At night the parched throat could be moistened and the heated body cooled; as the hot sand of the desert grew cold man and beast would sleep, refreshing themselves for the dry and scorching day that was to follow. Water was what these men sought and where there was water perhaps some of them might take root.

This hard and unyielding land bred a tough race of nomadic tribesmen who, with their women and children, had to be continuously on the move searching for the grazing they needed. These people were fiercely proud of their independence. They lived on their flocks and, though they might trade a little, few of them would settle in towns or on the corn-growing lands. The desert was their home and the tillers of the soil they held in scorn. In the course of generations some might change, but only some. They lived on the great trading routes and extorted taxes from the wealthy caravans that passed through their territories; they raided the rich lands that bordered them, but territorial gain was not their habit. They lacked cohesion because there was nothing to bind them, until in the later sixth century Mohammed propagated his militant religious beliefs. Faith then, as it has with so many people, bound them together and with a fanatical zeal they overran the Near East, Eastern Europe and the North African coast to and inclusive of Spain.

To the north of Canaan lay the mountainous country of the Hittites in what is now Turkish Anatolia. Intensely cold in winter and dry and hot in the summer months this country bred a hardy people. From the wool of their sheep they wove elaborate many-coloured clothes, and from the iron they found in their hills they fashioned their axes and spear heads. They were the natural outcome of their surroundings. They ravaged Canaan and it was only the greater strength of Babylon and Egypt that kept them in their place.

To the south, rich and fat on the waters of the Nile, lay Egypt. The Egyptians were skilled in all forms of craftmanship. They were wealthy and enjoyed a highly organized political system. Their pharaohs were mighty monarchs, their priests were powerful and their land-owning nobility loyal to both king and priest. All this gave stability to their society and enabled them to exercise control over the less advanced Syrian, Canaanite and Hebrew tribes to their north. They were rich in grain and cattle. Hemmed in on either side by desert, which for the most part was uninhabited, they were for many centuries free from outside interference.

Away to the east were the Assyrians and Babylonians. Unlike the Egyptians these people were constantly subjected to pressures and invasions from the Elamites, Medes, Persians and later Mongols. While the Egyptian kingdom remained a constant factor, power in the east was constantly changing hands.

Canaan was the bridge joining these great civilizations; in fact it was the only bridge and like an irresistible tide the peoples of the east on the one hand and the Egyptians on the other would sweep across its pleasant plains. When these invasions receded, or when their oppressors were otherwise preoccupied, the people of Canaan were free to develop their own small kingdom; but, however well established this might seem to be, sooner or later the rising tide from one flank or the other would once more engulf them.

The path of history is the journey of man; for, however great other influences may be, it is man who is the true architect of events. For no area is this more true than for Canaan, and thus no strategic analysis is complete without comment on the character of those men who controlled and influenced thought in this part of the world.

Though events will rise and fall in their importance with the comings and goings of kings and princes; though politicians and priests who were concerned with doctrine, cult and outside trappings will play their inevitable parts; and though good men and saints will supply a spiritual leaven and raise standards of philosophy, culture and thought; it is the thousands of men and women, ordinary folk either living on or by the land or in the cities, that provide mass opinion and that constitute the bricks and mortar of the state edifice. Without them nothing can be achieved; with them empires can be built; through them religious consciousness can develop or moral standards decay.

What manner of men then were those who dwelt in Canaan? They were reputed to have had fine physique—giants they were called, tall as cedars. They possessed many admirable qualities; but their most outstanding characteristic was their strong tribal instinct. This, though having its advantages, tended to narrow loyalties and to foment jealousies, failings from which at times they were grievously to suffer. Only when their unity was forged on the anvil of deep religious conviction could they achieve greatness. Such a time was during the period of David's kingship and again in the period of the Maccabees; but always the weakness inherent in the tribal system would come in to destroy hard-won achievements.

In spite of much that strikes one as very elementary in their way of life and indeed of their civilization, in searching through the records of this historical and deeply significant period, one cannot be but impressed with the parallels to our own times. The destruction of the kingdom of David, the decline that followed the extravagance of Solomon and his growing away from the masses, the sack of Jerusalem could all be repeated in our world today.

The strategic significance of Canaan derived from her geographic position; but it also was affected by the character, the fortitude as well as the weaknesses of her people. Militarily her importance was due to the fact that she lay athwart the great roadway from the Nile to the Euphrates, and later from Greece and Rome to both the east and Egypt. He who held the Hills of Samaria was, therefore, always liable to be involved in wars that were not necessarily of his own choosing. Her military position was somewhat analogous to that of the Low Countries in Western Europe, whose people have for so long found themselves caught up in struggles between the giants on either flank.

2 *The first of the patriarchs*

Of all the figures of the Old Testament Abraham is, perhaps, the most romantic, for his story is that of the birth of a nation.

Before tracing the exploits of this attractive character it is well to face up to the question as to whether he really existed at all. It is claimed that he represents a period of history by some, the formative period of the Hebrews, and that what befell Abraham was, in fact, what occurred to a people. It has also been said that, even if Abraham existed as a person, he and Abram were not one man who changed his name but two individuals separated by some five hundred years. The reasoning behind this theory was that Abraham was said to be an Amorite and, therefore, of the same stock as the Canaanites, whereas he was of Aramaean stock; but so far away is all this that we must inevitably rely on much that is legend. There are, nevertheless, some facts we know to be true. For instance we know that the name Abi Ramu or Abram occurs in Ur contracts of the period, and that the raids which I shall later discuss by the Elamites did take place in Canaan.

Whatever the doubts, for they are not much more than doubts, I have chosen to treat him as an Aramaean and as one character, and have discarded the theory that he never existed at all.

What of the times in which he was supposed to have lived? Somewhere about the second millennium the ancient and powerful Semitic kingdom that Sargon the Great founded on the

Euphrates commenced gradually to decay, and the fierce Elamite tribes to the east were casting envious eyes on the fair and rich lands of their weakening neighbour. In the year 2280 it is recorded that the Elamite king, Kadur Nakhkhunte, invaded the Tigris and Euphrates deltas, pillaging the cities, slaying the people and destroying the temples. The dynasty at Ur fell and the Semitic population was forced to move up into northern Assyria and beyond.

This was the time when one, Terah, a Semitic sheik, who claimed his descent direct from Shem, dwelt at Ur. He had three sons, of whom Abi Ramu or Abram was the eldest. The others were Nahor and Haran. Terah decided to leave Ur and marched north, nearly seven hundred miles, to the Land of Naharain and there, on a branch of the River Habor, at Haram, he settled. Not long after this Terah died and the head of the family was now Abram.

Abram was in the prime of life, of fine stature, dignified and proud of the stock from which he sprang. Possessing all the characteristics of a leader, he was single minded and once he had decided did not permit anything or anybody to deviate him from his course. Moreover, in battle he proved himself as skilful as he was relentless.

Drawn by some irresistible force to move on he journeyed westwards into the Land of Canaan. With his wife and his nephew, Lot, and his servants he marched towards the setting sun. He passed through Hamath on the beautiful Orontes river by the banks of which grew pink oleanders and tall green grasses, whose clear waters rushed in cascades of silver over the rounded stones and rocks in the river bed.

In response to some divine call, which the Old Testament refers to as the voice of God, he pressed on, halting only for a while at Shechem in the Plain of Morah. He continued south until he reached the highlands between Bethel and Ai and here he finally rested.

With his and Lot's retinue now very much increased he soon found the grazing was insufficient for them and the local people and quarrels broke out between the Perizzites and his own followers. Loath to allow the friction to spread into the family circle he proposed to Lot that they should separate giving to his relative the choice. If Lot wished to move east he would stay west of the Jordan and vice versa. The story goes that Lot chose to cross the river and so he moved into the Vale of Siddim where flourished the cities of Sodom and Gomorrah.

Standing on the hills where Jerusalem is today Abram gazed around from the rising of the sun to its setting. Here, he thought was a land fit for kings, something to cherish. Here, perhaps, in his mind was the shadowy thought of generations to come, even of the birth of a nation.

It was at this time that the Elamite king, Kutur-Lagomar, claiming suzerainty over Canaan, carried out a punitive expedition. The local kings had refused to pay the tribute due to him. Angered, Katur-Lagomar crossed the desert and attached the cities of Ashtaroth and Kariathain, continuing south he sacked Ezion Geber on the Gulf of Akabah, then he crossed the Wilderness of Param and attacked Kadesh Barnia. The kings of Sodom and Gomorrah joined battle with him in the Vale of Siddim. They were, however, ingloriously defeated and those that were left fled to the mountains. Kutur-Lagomar sacked their two cities and departed with many prisoners, among whom were Lot and his family.

When he heard of this Abram set out in pursuit. Hanging on to the Elamites he bided his time before disclosing his intentions. Eventually, in the vicinity of Dan, the opportunity for which he had been waiting arose. Attacking under cover of darkness from two directions at once he surprised his enemy throwing them into confusion. He continued to harry them until he had recovered all that had been lost, including his nephew Lot and all his family.

He had known there could be no question of his being able to defeat in open battle a force as strong as that of the Elamites. On the other hand he might, by surprise and vigour, succeed in rescuing his relatives and regaining their possessions. This became his objective. He appreciated the reward that comes from a surprise attack, particularly if this can be put in under cover of darkness and by one who is presumed to be of no serious military consequence. He took full advantage of the fact that he was familiar with the country and that the enemy was not. By dividing his force into two parts and attacking from two directions he could give the impression of greater strength than he possessed. His success was confirmed by a vigorous pursuit which was not pressed too far, but just far enough to achieve its object, the freeing of the prisoners and the regaining of the stolen property. In the confusion and under cover of darkness he would be able to disengage and make his get-away.

Here was a military appreciation and military lessons as applicable today as they were four thousand years ago.

Abram had by this action now established himself not only as a man of substance, but as a military leader and a loyal ally. His stature grew among his own followers as well as with his neighbours, the rulers of Sodom and Gomorrah.

When he died he was wealthy in gold and in silver, in camels, in sheep and in goats and asses; but he was still a nomad. He moved, as all his tribe did, where the grazing was best. It was after the destruction of Sodom and Gomorrah that he went south into the then friendly coastal country, and it was there that Isaac was born. It was there, also, that at Beer-Sheba he made a covenant with the local ruler, Abimelech, that the well which he had dug there should be his property for ever. It is this story, like that of the purchase of the field for the burial of Sarah, that indicates his wandering state. Except for this field and the well at Beer-Sheba he had no possessions in land. Nomad or not, he founded a people and a religion.

3 The flight from Egypt and the defeat at Hormah

It is not always easy with accuracy to align biblical periods in terms of known historical events. There are, however, well-defined happenings in Egyptian history by which one can, with some certainty, fix dates and happenings recorded in the Old Testament.

There was a period in the fifteenth and seventeenth centuries when the Hyksos ruled the country and during this period many migrated from Canaan into the Nile Valley. The Hyksos were subjected to Semitic influence which is borne out by many of their names. Their dynasty however eventually crumbled and a new and strong Egyptian pharaoh, Ahmosis I, believing in centralized control, did away with that section of the powerful landed nobility that had hitherto formed the substance of government and to whom he attributed Egyptian weakness. Under him the whole country became the personal state of the pharaoh; his principal minister was thus an important man, but nevertheless a servant; Ahmosis' principal minister may well have been a Hebrew, Joseph.

The biblical account of his whole family, driven south by famine, coming to Egypt in supplication to their younger brother, rings true. This, coupled with the migration of thousands of others who fled from the famine and deprivations of the fierce Kabiri tribes, produced a political crisis. Eventually Harmahab, who ruled in the fourteenth century fearing the ever increasing numbers of the Hebrews, ordered the extermination of every male babe.

At periods of great distress most peoples have produced leaders of moral fibre who, by their courage and sagacity, have rescued them from despotism and imbued them with courage and faith. Such a man, Moses, the story goes, was now born among the Hebrews in Egypt. Saved and adopted by pharaoh's daughter he was brought up in the palace. His attack on the Egyptian soldier and his having to flee the country could well be true. Later, when he heard that Harmahab was dead he decided to return. So, with his wife and small child, he set out on an ass to cross the dreary desert that separated him from his kinsmen.

After several vain attempts he eventually persuaded the Pharaoh to permit his people to go into the desert to perform their religious rites. His plan, however, was more ambitious and was indeed nothing less than a complete exodus. When their intentions became clear an army was sent in pursuit. The story of the crossing of the Red Sea and of its closing on the Egyptians is half legend and half truth. The route they took, although for certain not known, could well have taken them along the north coast of Sinai where there are large areas of marsh and water. Strong winds from the Mediterranean, which can rapidly build up in this area, would be sufficient to bring about a rise in water and thus account for the Egyptian discomfiture.

Nevertheless, whether they followed the northern route or the one to the south through the Wilderness of Zin, the long trek over the arid desert was a grim undertaking for a tired and undernourished people. Thousands of them, old and young, men and women, with their children, their sick and the lame, with their goats and their donkeys, their cooking pots and rough black tents must have looked a sorry sight. Hope, faith and the fear of what they had left behind alone could have buoyed them up.

Their first attempt to re-enter their beloved country was by the obvious route from the south. They seemed to have failed to realize that this might involve them in serious fighting. Their failure in this, their first battle, was a foregone conclusion; and, as one sees how they went about it, small is the wonder.

The tribes who occupied Canaan were warlike peoples experienced in battle and well armed with bows and arrow, sword and spear. They fought under their tribal chiefs, but against a common enemy, they would unite. The Hebrews, who for generations had stagnated as labourers, were not soldiers. Such arms as they possessed were of their own making and of the military art they knew little.

That Moses was alive to the dangers is certain. With clear and detailed instructions, he sent out spies to study the ground and to report on it; to observe the inhabitants and to report both on their strength and their weaknesses; whether they were nomadic or whether they lived in cities and fortified places.

The reports that came back were conflicting. As proof of the richness of the land they brought back branches of grape vines, but they also said that the people were numerically strong and of obvious vitality. At first, on hearing what they considered to be discouraging reports, the people turned on Moses, even going so far as to say that it had been better for them to return to Egypt than to continue this seemingly hopeless wandering in an inhospitable desert. Moses told them to have courage and faith and above all to hold fast. As a result of his appeals a reaction set in and, in a thoroughly inconsequential way, their panic and fear gave way to a desire to take the initiative. Moses counselled against this, saying he would not lead them on so foolhardy an enterprise. Against his advice, and without his leadership, they decided to advance into Canaan.

Kedesh Barna, where they were encamped, was in the desert on the edge of the Wilderness of Param. From here they marched north towards the foothills of southern Canaan. Unorganized and without a proper leader they pressed on until they reached the slopes of Mount Hor, a hill about eight hundred feet above sea level and lying on the south-east of the Dead Sea. The air was good to breathe and the scene, after the arid and dreary desert, was refreshing for tired eyes. But of military plan there was none, neither were they deployed to meet an attack should one develop, which they surely should have assumed. They continued their advance northwards, but on reaching Hormah they came under attack by the Amalakites from the north and by other tribes from the west. Their enemies had not been slow to observe their weakness and lack of proper organization. The combined attack, which was put in with skill and vigour, found the invaders completely unprepared and, put to rout, they were sent hurtling back to the desert from which they had so recently, so hopefully and so foolishly come.

This was a foolish enterprise, undertaken against the advice of their leader by a people neither adequately armed nor trained for the task. Their initial advance, because it was unopposed, led to a feeling of optimism which, in the event, was shown to be as unfounded as it was dangerous. In our own times we recall the disastrous allied landings in Norway in 1940. Inadequately trained English units, unprotected by proper air cover, marched south with great optimism. They met, as they were bound to, trained German troops and, like the Hebrews at Hormah, they had to withdraw. In each case the object was laudable, but that is not sufficient; in each case the outcome was as inevitable as it was predictable.

The reverse at Hormah so weakened the Hebrews and so lowered their morale that it was not until a new generation had grown up that they were again fit to undertake warlike operations. It was a sad commencement to what was ultimately to prove a glorious campaign.

From Kedesh Barna where there was water, after resting, they slowly wandered across the desert, eventually trekking northwards to the Land of Moab, through which they hoped their passage would be peaceful. This was not to be, for the rulers of Giliad and of Bashan came out to meet them. By now, however, they had learned much, were far fitter and better trained. In the fights that ensued they scored signal successes and the king of the Ammonites and Og, king of Bashan, were slain. These victories meant that they were able to pass on unmolested, and the military significance was that they had a secure line of communication with no threat to their rear. They now had undisputed possession of the Mountains of Moab and the Heights of Ammon.

Moses, now an old man, slowly walked up the slopes of Mount Nebo from where he could gaze across at the Promised Land, the land he was not destined to enter. In the clear, fresh air he looked down on the deep salt waters of the Dead Sea and further on to the dark, brown mass of the Mountains of Judaea; at his feet the road ran steeply to the River Jordan beyond which he gazed at Jericho, just a small green oasis at the foot of the great hills beyond; while away to the north in the clear sky he saw the white cap of Mount Hermon.

He knew that his life span was drawing to its close and that the crossing would be undertaken by his successor, Joshua, the son of Nun, whom he had prepared for the responsibility. Moses had not only proved himself a great spiritual leader, he had shown that he was an outstanding soldier.

4 The battles of Jericho and Ai

Joshua's character, forged in the hard and unyielding desert, was strong and uncompromising. The tribes were now disciplined, ripe for action and, encouraged by their recent successes, impatient to cross the river and once again to enter Canaan, this time to stay. All they wanted was forthright and skilful leadership. Joshua provided this. His successes as a military leader mark him out as one of the great captains of history. In this chapter it will be seen how richly he deserves this assessment.

Canaan was divided into innumerable small realms among which there was little or no cohesion. In the coastal plain only did the Egyptians, who still claimed suzerainty over the whole country, exercise any real control. Local rulers, who were little more than tribal chiefs, had small bands of warriors, for the most part consisting of infantry who were generally armed with the sword and spear. They were physically hardy and in the defence of their own areas sometimes fanatically brave. Lack of centralized control was their principal weakness, making them vulnerable to piecemeal attack. With Egyptian influence negligible and Canaan disunited, the time for invasion was indeed propitious.

From over the deep valley to the rugged hills beyond, a distance of over twenty miles, the task seemed formidable. The power to manoeuvre was limited for, with the Jordan in flood

as it was at this time of the year when the snows on Hermon
were melting, there was no alternative to the crossing at the
ford in the Shittim Valley on the road to Jericho. Between here
and the far-off hills lay the fortified city of Jericho, the capture
of which must form the basis of any plan. From the fortress the
road led up to Michmash and thence on to the highlands about
Ephraim. The crossing of the river, the capture of Jericho and
the seizure of the heights beyond were thus the three phases of
Joshua's strategy.

Before moving he sent two men down from his camp to
reconnoitre the crossings, the road to Jericho and the city itself.
So it was that, on a hot and sultry night, two young men sat by
the ford over the river on the road to Jericho. They were sun-
tanned, hardy and keen-looking men. Coming down from
heights of Ammon where the air had been fresh and invigorating, they found the low Jordan Valley, here well below sea
level, sultry and oppressive. The sweat poured from the two as
they sat in the moonlight; but at least they were on the
threshold of Canaan, the land of their dreams. Only standing
in their path to the uplands and the lush plains beyond lay the
city of Jericho. How strong would it prove to be, how well
would it be defended, and what manner of men were its people?
These were the questions to which they had to find the answer.

The immediate landscape looked horribly inhospitable. The
actual river was not broad at this point, but the valley through
which it wound its sluggish way was. Close in on either side of
the rough road was a reedy swamp and, except at the ford, the
banks were almost unusable. Time and the rains roaring down
from the mountains beyond had worn away the soft whitish
soil of the foothills into a myriad of needle-like hills and ridges,
so close together that passage across them would be almost
impossible. Gleaming white in the pale light of the moon they
looked like devils' teeth. Beyond this eerie scene and about ten
miles on lay the walled city which was their goal, tucked in at the
foot of the mountains that formed the watershed of the river
and the main backbone of the Canaan highlands. The same
road and the same scene exist today, except that in place of the

ford there is now a bridge and the road is well surfaced. So, were we to look across the river as these two men did, we should see much the same sight as met their gaze. It was obvious to the two that here was a place to guard.

There were no sentries and so it seemed the people of Jericho must be idle and seemingly unprepared. The two went on. Their entry into the city was easy and they mistakenly supposed unobserved. Looking for somewhere to rest they found the house of one Rahab, a harlot. From her they learned much. She told them that the people were disunited and that they had little stomach for fighting. They had heard stories of the strength of the tribes and of their great journey across the desert, of how their god had helped them and of the drying up of the sea and of the waters drowning their pursuers; they had also heard of and were deeply impressed, by their victories over the rulers beyond the Jordan.

That the entry of the two spies had not passed unobserved was soon evidenced by the arrival of the king's guard at Rahab's house. She, hiding her two visitors under the grass drying on her roof, denied their presence, saying that she had seen them but neither knew from whence they had come nor where they were going. They had gone towards the gate, she continued, and it should be simple to overtake them. When the guard had departed she extracted a promise from the two that when their army arrived her house and all her family would be spared. This promise was given and in the event was kept. That night, letting them down by a rope over the city wall, she helped them to make their escape.

On hearing the report from the spies Joshua decided to assault at once. This, according to the biblical narrative he did with a force of some forty thousand men, though this may indeed be inaccurate and exaggerated. It is difficult to assess the strength of the men of Jericho, but it was probably not more than a few thousand. Nevertheless, their position was a strong one and their power to resist a siege would have been considerable. A long investment, during which the enemy might be reinforced was the last thing Joshua wanted. He decided to base his plan on the low morale of the people and reckoned that a great show of force would in all probability sap what little will to fight they had.

This was how he went about it. His army would march around the city to show its strength. This it would do for six days and on the seventh all his men would give a great shout. The ark, their sacred emblem, was to be carried before them, as colours were with us in later times. We read that on the great shout the walls fell flat and so the army entered, every man going straight before him.

My interpretation of the falling of the walls of Jericho was that it was in fact the crumbling of the will of the inhabitants to fight. The victory was due to the exploitation of the fifth column element and the excellent intelligence reports Joshua had received. It showed Joshua to be a shrewd leader, confident not only in his cause but in his own judgement. The moment was critical, his people had suffered much and their first attempt to enter Canaan had been a tragic failure. This must not be repeated. If he quickly followed up the recent victories in Moab he could ride on the crest of their justified confidence.

Once across the Jordan and with Jericho subdued, his next step was to obtain a firm foothold on the hills beyond. From Jericho the road to the highlands above followed a steep gorge to Michmash, beyond which opened the Wilderness of Beth-aven and here, looking down on the valley, stood the city of Ai. Here the great central range of Canaan was at its narrowest, and he who held Ai possessed the key to an important route from the Jordan to the coastal plain.

Unfortunately success sometimes brings with it a carelessness and disregard of the fighting qualities of an opponent. The advantages of moving rapidly after a successful engagement must be nicely balanced against the risks that are involved, and a too precipitate haste may lead to an unwelcome reverse. This was to prove only too true in the first assault on Ai.

Joshua naturally sent out reconnaissance parties. Because a commander must be guided in his decisions by the reports he receives from them it is imperative that the questions to which he wants answers are abundantly clear. He also must let the men he sends know his fears if any. Finally such men must be those in whose judgement he has implicit confidence. Whether or not Joshua followed these age-old rules we shall see.

Let us, therefore, climb up with these men from the hot and sultry valley and stand with them as they reached the invigorating heights above. Rugged tree-covered hills and deep green valleys stretched north as far as the eye could see. The mountain ranges ran on it seemed endlessly and the city of Ai did not look too impressive. So, when the men returned, they said that Ai should not present a serious problem. In their estimation two thousand or so men would be sufficient for the task, and in the meantime the remainder could follow slowly as they were ready. Their estimate was that the men of Ai were few.

Optimism and wishful thinking had swayed their judgement; but in fairness to them it must be remembered that these men had only recently had evidence of the rot that had set in and been the cause of the downfall of Jericho. What they did not appreciate was that they were now up against a hardy hill people, well versed in war and ready to fight and to do this with both skill and determination.

The report was accepted and so a small force was despatched for the task. This was to be an unfortunate affair, for the men of Ai came out to meet them and utterly surprised them by the ferocity of their attack. The tribesmen were routed, their proud advance ending in an inglorious flight. It was a sad affair in which they sustained only some thirty-odd casualties.

This set-back was bred of over-confidence, of conceit and a gross underestimate of their foe. It is now that we see Joshua at his best. First, he prayed asking forgiveness and seeking inspiration; second, he did not deviate from his object; and third, he learned his lesson. No longer underestimating his opponent he concentrated superior forces for his next assault, combining this with an outflanking movement and an attack from the rear. Every detail was meticulously thought out before battle was joined; signals were arranged and the exact part each element of his force was to play was most carefully planned.

A direct assault on the city would be costly and there would be little chance of a siege resulting in capitulation. Perhaps the circumstances of the recent reverse could be turned to good account? The canopy of night could be used to achieve surprise, and guile could be employed to draw the enemy out on to ground of Joshua's own choosing. All these thoughts went through the leader's head and were used to form the basis of a model plan of which the details were as follows.

Under cover of darkness he despatched a large and carefully picked force with instructions to post themselves in rear of Ai. The main body was to advance on the city by daylight and this force would, when the soldiers came out to meet them, feign retreat and withdraw into the wilderness. By this stratetem he would denude the place of its garrison and leave it open to assault from the rear. For success this plan depended on meticulous timing and the attack from the rear was not to be until he, Joshua, had himself given the signal. The assault from the rear was to coincide with that of an outflanking movement, the troops for which were under his direct command.

When the force for the attack in the rear was in position and the main body in readiness to advance, Joshua led the outflanking party into the valley by which they were to approach. When, with the first light of dawn, the enemy saw the Hebrew host approaching the city they forthwith went out again to do battle. Acting according to their orders the tribesmen turned and fled towards the wilderness and they were, as Joshua had expected, hotly pursued. Then it was that he gave the expected signal by raising his spear and pointing it towards Ai. The men in ambush arose, entered the city which they set on fire. This was the signal for the main body to turn and fight. The enemy, seeing their town in flames in their rear, became demoralized. In the ensuing fight they were routed and great was the slaughter.

A good tactical plan should aim at deceiving the enemy and, at the same time, it should be simple to execute. If envelopment is combined with frontal action the proper timing of the two movements in the operation is of the utmost importance.

Control of this timing must rest in the hands of the commander and not left to some fixed hour, for if it is, the unforeseen cannot be catered for. The commander must, however, be where he can exercise this control and his judgement of the critical moment must be sure. Joshua's plan fulfilled all these conditions. More than this, he made the fullest use of darkness to cover and to complete his preliminary moves. Finally, and by no means least important, the discipline and training of his troops was good enough to stand up to the strain such an operation would demand of them.

The Battle of Ai was a splendid success which had the most far-reaching results. First, it ensured the commander the respect and confidence of his troops; second, it gave him a strong position for his negotiations with the neighbouring Gibeonite tribes; and third, it gave him a secure base for his subsequent operations.

He now marched south towards Gaza which he captured and, continuing his advance he marched on Hebron, finally completing the circle by returning to his base. He had, by a spectacular series of victories, established a strong position in the whole of southern Canaan and was free to turn his attention to the north.

Joshua, by his upbringing as well as by his natural instincts was a deeply religious man and his faith was the mainspring of his innate confidence. Like King Arthur, he may indeed have been a romantic character of mythological history; but surely there is little reason to believe that the detailed stories of his exploits, handed down over the centuries, are not basically true. There is surely no valid cause to doubt his existence, even though there is ample evidence that the 'Hebrew invasion' was not completed so quickly as reported nor confined to a single campaign. At the same time I can see no reason why we can logically deny either the assault on Jericho or the attack on Ai.

As a military commander Joshua showed qualities of discernment, understanding both the strength and the weaknesses of those who he was leading. He had the invaluable knack of being able to fathom the enemy's mind. If he failed in this respect on his first assault he was quick to learn from his mistake. In tactics he made the fullest use of the factor of surprise and guile to deceive the enemy. Though he planned in great detail he after making his plan clear to his subordinates left the execution of it to them. In neither the political nor the military field did he ever shrink from a bold plan.

He stands in history as a great man on any count.

5 The defeat of Sisera

The original and superficially tidy settlement of the tribes of
Joshua, so graphically depicted on the maps with which we
are familiar, give a false impression of the true state of affairs in
Canaan at this time. The migration of the Hebrews and their
incursion into the bordering countries was, in fact, a process
that took place over a very prolonged period. At the time with
which we are now about to deal they certainly were not in
possession of the whole country, large areas of which were
occupied by Canaanite people. Neither had they any political
unity; they had no king and, after Joshua, no leader. They were
a loose confederation of semi-nomads of common stock, who
had settled in an untidy patchwork among an indigenous
population. They were held together by the bond of religion, of
which the Ark and the covenant of circumcision were the
symbols.

Sometimes the pressures from local Canaanite tribes was
intolerable. Such an occasion was when one Jabin, who assumed
the title of King of all Canaan, assembled an army in the Plain
of Esdraelon, under the command of his general, Sisera.

There then dwelt, on the slopes of Mount Ephraim, a
Hebrew prophetess named Deborah. Realizing the threat from
Sisera's army she called on the people to take action, reminding
them of their past and how Moses and Joshua had, by resolute
action, saved them. Her appeals were unheeded by many.

As is so often the case, the further men are from the source of danger the less do they care; so it was that only the tribes in the north rallied. The Ephraimites and the Benjamites responded as did the tribes of Manasseh, Zebulun, Issacher and the children of Napthali. Reuben would not heed her call nor would Gilead cross the Jordan, the men of Dan on the coast remained in their ships and the tribes of Levi, Simeon and Judah all failed her. Nevertheless, from the six tribes who did support her, she managed to assemble an army of ten thousand men whom she placed under the command of Barak, a hitherto untried general in war.

In the battle that was fought terrain played a vital part in both the strategy Deborah and Barak adopted and in the manner in which the tactics of the battle developed. Northern and southern Canaan were effectively separated by the great Carmel Ridge which, springing from Mount Gilboa and the Heights of Ephraim, ran north-west until it dropped precipitously into the Mediterranean. To the north lay an extensive plain which ran from the sea to the River Jordan. It was bounded on the north by the Hills of Galilee, the Hills of Morah, and the whole was divided by natural features into three distinct parts; these were, the coastal plain of Plain of Accho, the Plain of Esdraelon and finally the Vale of Jezreel.

The Plain of Accho was separated from Esdraelon by a spur of the Hills of Galilee which terminated in the vicinity of Harosheth about a hundred yards from the steep slopes of Carmel. This gap and the lower slopes of the Hills of Galilee formed the only practical approach to the coastal plain from southern Canaan. It was of considerable military significance throughout biblical times and was used by Napoleon when he laid siege to Acre. Through this narrow defile ran the River Kishon which meandered across the southern part of Esdraelon. Looking north from Megiddo on the Carmel Ridge one surveyed a vast inland basin of rich arable soil which, after rain, became a veritable bog and over which movement by vehicles was virtually impossible. The Kishon, hardly visible, was a sluggish stream only a few feet wide. Here and there were clumps of trees to show where some well was worked to water the small orchards. At other places dark patches of reeds indicated areas of swamp. Between the Carmel Ridge and the Hills of Galilee an isolated hill, Mount Tabor, stood like a fortress guarding the road to the Sea of Galilee and the north.

Now for the battle itself. Sisera had taken up a strong position at Harosheth. His force consisted of over ten thousand infantry and nine hundred chariots of iron. He was, in modern terms, strong in armour. In contrast, the army which Deborah and Barak had collected had no chariots and was entirely composed of infantry, who were armed with the bow and arrow and the sword. To attempt to attack Sisera would have been folly, for once the assaulting infantry were committed they would fall an easy prey to counter-attack by Sisera's iron chariots. Deborah was not to be tempted into such rash action; instead she took up a defensive position on the slopes of Mount Tabor, thus placing her army between Jabin, at Hazor by the waters of Morom, and his troops at Harosheth. This gave her command over the road to the north. By this means she placed the responsibility for attacking on the Canaanites which automatically passed the initiative to her. Her position on Tabor was easy to defend, the approaches being devoid of cover. Moreover, it enabled her to give battle on ground of her own choosing.

One, Heber, in some way related to Moses, but who had severed himself from the tribes, played into her hands, for he told Sisera of the details of the Hebrew positions. The Canaanite, confident of his strength, made the cardinal mistake of coming out from his strong position into the open plain.

As his army advanced Deborah and Barak watched while the ever lengthening line of chariots drew out from the western angle of the Harosheth defile. It must have been an inspiring sight, this massive force moving slowly across the open plain. When they passed Megiddo they wheeled north and advanced on Tabor, at which juncture, as though by a divine providence, the rain commenced to fall. The whole area was soon a sea of mud and in such a state that it was impossible for the chariots to manoeuvre.

Now was Deborah's chance. Her men charged down with a fierce highland ferocity into the plain amidst Sisera's bogged vehicles. The attack was delivered with such élan upon the labouring charioteers that the Canaanites fled, some going east into the Vale of Jezreel and some west to the coastal plain. Their chariots, bogged down in the mud, were abandoned and left upon the field. The remnants of this once confident host were pursued to Harosheth. Those who did not fall by the sword were drowned in the River Kishon.

Sisera, as soon as he saw how the battle was going fled the field, seeking shelter with Jael, the wife of Heber, who seeing his plight took him in. Whilst he rested she covered him with a mantle and drove a nail through his brain. So, as Deborah had prophesized, he died at the hand of a woman.

This battle is of considerable interest to the student of war. The tactics employed highlighted the relative importance of defence and attack; in this case it showed the price that has to be paid when offensive operations are undertaken in conditions unpropitious to the attacker and favourable to the defence. Sisera's mistake has often been repeated and, generally, with the same results. His second error was to commit his mobile troops to action on terrain unsuited to them. The strength of his position at Harosheth lay not only in its situation at the head of an important pass, but in the difficulties that must face any attacker. Much the same applied to Mount Tabor. The fundamental difference lay in the fact that Sisera had a strong force of chariots; and, had he used his infantry to assault the Tabor position and kept his chariots in reserve, possible on the harder and slightly higher ground near Shunem, he might have been able to destroy the Hebrews when they left their strong position in their headlong counter-attack. Deborah was fortunate in that the weather played into her hands; but this factor should surely have entered Sisera's calculations, for he knew the country. In Deborah's counter-attack timing was important; for the enemy had to be fully committed before it was launched.

Military history is littered with examples of these factors. In modern times there is the classic of General Montgomery's defence at Alem Halfa. Here he drew Rommel's teeth by letting the German armour, almost inviting the armour, to attack in circumstances which favoured the British defence, Rommel's losses in tanks were heavy and the British negligible; in this manner was the balance of armour as between the Germans and the British redressed and the way paved for the subsequent offensive at Alamein.

In the Peninsular campaign, after a successful engagement, Wellington withdrew his forces to the now famous Lines of Torres Vedras where he drew the French on to attack him on ground of his own choosing when he could give battle as he wanted it. The French were soundly defeated and this, again, was a prelude to an offensive that led to the ultimate winning of the campaign. This was a favourite tactical concept of Wellington which he once more applied at Waterloo.

In reverse there is the sad story of King Harold at Senlac when a too precipitous counter-attack led to defeat. Had Harold's men been held in control, after he himself had been hit by an arrow, they would never have fallen victims to the Norman knights as they did. Defeat and conquest was the price they had to pay for sallying out into the open plain, unsuited to them but affording ideal conditions for the mounted Norman knights.

To Deborah must go the glory. She inspired the tribes, planned the campaign and, by winning this victory, made her countrymen at least for a time a force to be reckoned with. The land had peace for forty years. Of Sisera's death at Jael's hand this much must be said; it was a fitting end to a commander who deserts his men in their hour of need.

6 Gideon's victory over the Midianites

The first reference to the Midianites was when Moses sought shelter with them and they were well disposed and actively friendly to the Hebrews. However, in the fulness of time this rather small nomadic tribe had expanded into a people of considerable size. Born and bred in the desert they were a fierce and warrior-like race. As they expanded they naturally sought pastures new and it was inevitable that they should push their way into the Moabite territories to their north. This small movement eventually gave way to a far more serious situation when the Midianites overflowed first into Ammon and then into Gilead, finally spreading over the Jordan into Jezreel. At first they came only for grazing, but later they pushed their way into the heart of the country over which they sprawled about in large encampments. At the time of this story of all the tribal areas only Gilboa and Ephraim were free of them.

Since Deborah's victory over Sisera the tribes had tended to drift away from the worship of Yahweh and many had turned to Baal. Politically there was still little or no cohesion among them and they sorely felt the need of spiritual and military leadership.

Fear is a wonderful stimulant when cohesion is lacking and fear of the Midianites was drawing the tribes together again. It was for this reason that they called on one, Gideon, the son of Joash, to be their king, a title which when offered to him he would not accept. Gideon had already shown the stuff he was

made of in an incident that concerned his father, a worshipper
of Baal and a high priest of the heathen god, whose idol was in
his keeping. Incensed, Gideon, in company with about twenty
young men, had raided and demolished the idol and the grove
of trees in which it stood. Among a strongly superstitious people
this was no mean thing to do and, as might be supposed, many
quickly cried for his blood in vengeance. Strangely it was his
father's skilful pleading that saved his life.

Nevertheless, Gideon's popularity increased and the loyal
tribes elected him as their leader to deal with the Midianite
menace. His call to arms met with an unexpectedly good
response; but, when he saw the motley he had collected, he
knew this was not what he wanted. He would be far better off
and far more likely to achieve his object with a smaller, well
selected and purposeful body of men than with an uncertain
and unwieldy mob. The first thing was to get rid of the faint-
hearted. When he told those who were not wholeheartedly with
him to return to their tents large numbers drifted away. Nevertheless, he was not yet satisfied. To understand why and how
he still further reduced his numbers it is necessary first to
describe the relative positions of his and the Midianite forces.

His men were assembled on Mount Gilboa and opposite
them, not more than a mile or so away, were the Midianites.
Available to Gideon's men there were only three sources of
drinking water; one by the village of Jezreel and one out on the
open plain, the third and only safe one to approach was a stream
which ran from the Well of Herod, close under the slopes of
Gilboa. The stream was of some size with a considerable
volume of water, its deep bed and soft banks made it a
formidable obstacle and the protection this afforded Gideon's
men was an important factor. Unfortunately the reeds and
undergrowth, whilst affording cover to those wishing to drink,
could also give protection to an approaching enemy. It was this
that influenced Gideon in his method of sorting out the alert
and intelligent from the dull and unimaginative.

He sent all down to the stream to drink. Those who bowed
themselves down on their knees to drink did not appreciate the

danger of their position; whilst those who crouched, lapping up
the water with one hand as they held their spears with the other,
keeping their eyes open for the enemy, were alert, keen and
intelligent. Such men were not likely to be caught by surprise,
and Gideon's intended tactics called for alert and not careless
soldiers. By this method he chose three hundred on whose
qualities he could rely.

Before he put the finishing touches to his plan he wanted to
know more about the foe. What were their intentions and of
what were they thinking? What was the state of their morale
and what did they think of his tribesmen? How were they
armed and what proportion of them was really good fighting
material? To find out for himself under cover of darkness he
visited their camp and listened to the talk among the guards.
He heard one tell his companions of a dream he had had and
from this he discovered that they thought he had a far bigger
army than was the case and it was also obvious that the fact of
his having whittled his force down to a mere three hundred had
not reached them. He now knew that to counter-balance his
small numbers he had superiority in morale. This he should
exploit, to which end he must work on Midianite superstitions
and fears. He would, therefore, base his plan on surprise which
he could only achieve if he attacked at night. He devised a plan
which for originality and daring is surely unequalled.

Imagine Gideon as he unfolded this to his followers. He
must have known there would be scepticism and the only way
to overcome this would be by a candid approach. He first told
them of his reconnaissance and of all that he had overheard,
explaining the state of mind of the enemy and the reasons for his
belief that their morale was low. He then must logically have
underlined how much surprise was of the essence of his plan,
and why he must, therefore, put in his attack at night and without delay. To get his timings right the attack should start at
the beginning of the middle watch. To deceive his enemy as to
his real strength he would divide his force into small columns
thus giving the impression of greater numbers then he possessed. Each man was to carry an earthenware pot in which was to

be concealed a lamp and all were to carry trumpets. Continuing, he told them to look to him and do as he did. When he blew on his trumpet every man on all sides of the enemy camp was to blow on his trumpet and then to break his pitcher, shouting, 'The sword of the Lord and of Gideon.'

And so, each man knowing what he was to do, the columns moved silently in the darkness and converged on the sleeping Midianites. Suddenly the stillness of the night was shattered as the three hundred blew on their trumpets and, breaking their pitchers, held their lamps high in their left hands, shouting, 'The sword of the Lord and of Gideon.' In the darkness there was confusion, uncertainty, plus the fear that they were all surrounded. Animals stampeded, camp followers ran here and there and women screamed, in the dark each man's sword was drawn against his comrade. Panic-stricken they fled down the valley, past Beth-Shittah to Zererath near Beth-Shean, and on to the lip of Abelmeholah, the deep bank over which the Vale of Jezreel falls into the Jordan. With Gideon's men in pursuit the flight continued.

Tactical victories of this type can only be turned into successes if the beaten enemy is relentlessly pursued. His plight is almost certain to be worse than that of the pursuer, tired though he may be. Gideon's success brought the neighbouring tribes into the fight and as he followed the enemy into the Hills of Gilead he was joined by those east of the river. In spite of fatigue he drove his men on and, finally coming up with all that was left of the Midianites, he took their kings prisoners.

This miraculous success was due to skill, courage and, perhaps above all, to faith. Skill in devising a bold plan that completely surprised the enemy and also played on their superstitions and fears; it was bold and the risks that were inherent in it he readily accepted; it demanded faith in his god which reflected itself in the faith Gideon had in himself. In selecting his men he applied an intelligence test that would indicate an attitude of mind which in war is always of greater importance then mere physical strength. He knew that a few well-chosen men, hand-picked for their qualities of alertness, are worth more than many thousands lacking cohesion and discipline and devoid of that courage and intelligence which mean so much in battle.

His relentless pursuit put the seal of greatness on his leadership. He was able to drive those tired men on to victory because of the confidence they had in him. The will to fight, physical and mental fitness, discipline and faith in the cause and the leadership are as important now, even in this atomic and so-called push-button age, as they were three thousand years ago.

7 *The heroes*

Deborah's defeat of Sisera and Gideon's victory over the Midianites had marked a turning point in the local Hebrew contests. Nevertheless to the south they were now threatened by a new danger of aggression from the firmly established Philistine tribes, who were not in the strict sense of the word a nation, rather were they a closely confederated tribal system, well organized and well armed and who could and did act with a unity unpractised by the Hebrews. The latter were still suffering from internal differences and selfish tribal interests with little or no cohesion, which weakness told seriously against them in their resistance to the ever-expanding ambitions of their neighbours. Philistine incursions into the heart of Judaea was now becoming a threat to the very existence of the whole Hebrew community.

This brought about an awareness of their weakness and heralded a new and a great period in their political development —the period of the Kings. The times were marked by individual acts of bravery—epics of heroism. Of the many stories of this era, two stand out; each differing from the other, yet each having its peculiar appeal and its own message.

The first is that of Jonathan at Michmash. Jonathan, the son of Saul, was one of those figures in history around whom romance attaches. His chivalry reminds one of the Knights of the Round Table and of Edward the Black Prince. His friendship with David, which amounted to something of a brotherly love, in the face of his father's jealousy and hatred, was a mark of the steadfastness of this man; but it was his exploit at Michmash that indicated in clear relief not only his personal gallantry, but also his tactical resourcefulness.

The Philistines had pushed deep into the tribal areas. They occupied most of Judaea and had placed a garrison at Michmash, the importance of which was that it guarded the road to the centre of the country from the Jordan valley, the same road that Joshua traversed when he marched on Ai.

Saul's army was at Seneh (so called for the thorns upon its trees) which lay on the south side of the Michmash gorge. The Philistine position was a naturally strong one which it would have been beyond the power of Saul's force to take. In order to make the Philistine garrison vulnerable to attack Jonathan conceived a plan as daring as it was effective, the basis of which was to surprise and confuse. Surprise and the consequent disorder that this could create was the cardinal point, therefore any form of conventional approach must be discarded. It was for this reason that he decided to carry out the plan single handed, accompanied only by his servant. For sheer audacity, with odds against him that would sober most men, this surely was unsurpassed.

The Philistine camp could be entered by a narrow defile between two rocks, just beyond which was a small plateau on which the outpost or guard was posted. In the stillness of the night he and his man bearing his arms crawled up between the rocks and, emerging on the plateau, they showed themselves to the guard. On seeing them the Philistines laughed, taunting them with having come out of the caves in which they had been hiding. They told them to come up and be taught a thing or two. Jonathan and his man edged slowly forward and suddenly, taking the guard by surprise, they attacked, killing twenty men. At this point they were assisted by a divine providence in the form of a sudden violent thunderstorm which added to the general chaos. The rest of the garrison, unaware of what the two had done, thought that some quarrel had broken out among their own people and in the confusion created by the storm, commenced fighting among themselves. Saul's men, who were waiting near at hand, now attacked; so, too, did many others who had come in from the surrounding hills. Michmash was captured and so effective was the rout that Saul pursued the remnants of the garrison over the hill and down as far as the coastal plain.

In war the element of surprise is possibly the most important factor. Wolfe surprised General Montcalm at Quebec. There was in his plan one of the elements of Jonathan's ruse—the use of an unexpected and invisible line of approach. In the American Civil War Stonewall Jackson surprised Banks when, in his advance on Winchester, he took the unexpected line of approach along the Lauray Fork. The raids of the Long Range Desert Group in the last war frequently achieved outstanding success and they, too, relied on surprise. These raids had something in common with that of Jonathan; they struck right deep into the enemy camp and were carried out by a handful of men against vastly superior numbers. The usefulness of such actions is dubious unless they form part of a larger plan; and this is precisely what Jonathan's exploit did. Finally, and probably most interesting of all, in Allenby's campaign in Palestine in the First World War one of his brigades used this very same stratagem which was inspired by the story as told in the Bible. Patrols were sent out to find out if this route did in fact exist and they found the gap as described between the two great rocks. On this the plan was altered and, instead of mounting a brigade attack, one company only moved up in the dark and reaching the small flat plateau where Jonathan stood facing the Philistines, they found and surprised the Turkish garrison, which, in disorder, took to its heels.

The second story concerns David's fight with Goliath. David, at that time a mere shepherd boy, was ruddy and of fair complexion and possibly fifteen years of age. Saul had been king of Israel for some years and the war against the Philistines was at its height.

The field on which the drama was acted lay in the Shephelah, the name given to the lower ridges and spurs of the Judaean highlands. It was a great battle ground in Canaan's history and at this time a debatable stretch of territory between the Philistines and the Israelites. Running up from the coastal plain through these low hills were many valleys which were of considerable military significance to fortress Judah. The Philistines used the Vale of Ajlon, the northern of these, in their advance to Michmash and it was down this same valley that Saul and Jonathan pursued them after the defeat of the garrison. To the south of this ran the Vale of Sorak and further south still, just above Ashdod, was the Vale of Elah which reached deep into Judah and opened up the strategically important high ground about Hebron.

It was at Shocoth in this valley that the Philistine army was now drawn up in fighting array. On the far side lay Saul's force. Shocoth was a naturally strong position being isolated from the rest of the ridge. In order to attach the Israelites the Philistines would, however, themselves have had to cross a level stretch of land, ford the main stream and then cross two further wadies and, for the final assault, they would have had to climb the open slopes leading to Saul's position. It was these factors of topography that give the most reasonable explanation for the long hesitation on the part of both armies to come to grips.

The level piece of ground between the two forces provided the stage for David's encounter with Goliath. The idea of resorting to champions was not an unusual one and in the case of the Philistines with Goliath as their champion they had an unbeaten hero and a veritable giant. Saul had no one who seemed prepared to accept the challenge.

Sent to the Israelite camp by his father with food and provisions for his elder brothers, David arrived at this critical moment. He was appalled at the craven fear that Goliath had apparently instilled into all. His outburst merely brought forth the ridicule of his brothers and of the soldiery; but Saul heard of it and sent for him. To the king, David, quite unawed, said he would go and fight the Philistine.

He disdained the armour which Saul had offered him because

it was too heavy and was, moreover, unsuited to his intention and also, he said, he had not yet proved himself worthy to wear it. He armed himself instead with a sling and six round stones. Thus equipped he was ready to walk out to meet what must have appeared to so many as certain death. But he knew he possessed something Goliath lacked; in modern terms it was fire power, coupled with the courage, the skill and the brains to use it.

Goliath looked magnificent. He wore a helmet of brass, his body was encased in a coat of mail and his legs were protected by shining brass plates. The staff of his spear was like a weaver's beam and he carried a mighty sword. A man bearing his shield went before him. As Goliath approached, full of proud confidence, believing in the advantage of his physical strength, David stood his ground. When near enough he aimed one stone from his sling which struck the giant on the temple. As he fell David seized his sword and drawing it out from its mighty sheath with one blow he cut off Goliath's head. When the Philistines saw the fate of their champion they fled. Saul and his men rose with a mighty shout and pursued them as far as the gates of Ekron.

The lesson David taught the world was that righteous indignation against an aggressor is justified only when one has the courage and the faith to stand and fight. It has also taught us that intelligence is of greater importance than massive strength which can be brought to the ground by the skilfully applied fire of even small weapons. Indeed, the history of the tactical battle is to no small extent the history of the proper application of fire power.

Sometimes in modern life we are apt to feel there is not much room for heroics, but one has only to think of the great individualists who pioneered in the world of aviation, of those who have singly parachuted into danger for a cause in which they believed, and of the many men and women who have risked all in a resistance movement when terrorized by hostile occupation. We still have our heroes and it is they who really set the pace, give the example and, for the rest of us, show the way.

Jonathan and David did just this.

8 Saul's campaigns and defeat at Gilboa

We are now about to enter a great period in Hebrew history, that of the Kings. That a people so highly tribal and individualistic should become a united kingdom, a kingdom destined to leave its mark on the pages of history, was due to the emergence of certain strong characters, great men judged by any standards. In spite of this, however, their achievements were only possible because the peoples of the Nile and the Euphrates were in temporary decline or otherwise occupied.

Although Assyria had awakened from slumber and had under King Tiglath-Pileser I invaded Syria and ravaged parts of Canaan, The Assyrians neither occupied nor attempted to impose political control over the land. The invasions had been for plunder and not conquest.

Egypt was in a state of wretched decline. In spite of the fact that she had nominal suzerainty over Canaan some indication of the depth to which she had sunk can be gleaned from the pathetic story of Winammon, the emissary of Rameses XII. He was sent to a Phoenician prince in the Lebanon to secure cedar wood for the temple of Amon, was subjected to every form of indignity and was, indeed, fortunate to escape with his life. He received his first shock when his vessel put in to a small port called Dor, a few miles to the south of Mount Carmel. This was the city of a small Philistine tribe, the Thekels, who came from Crete. Here he was robbed not only of all his money but also of his credentials. Only after interminable delays and many indignities did he manage to collect a bag of silver in compensation for his losses. Depleted of most of his money and without his credentials he reached Byblos at the foot of Mount Hermon where he obtained an audience with the prince who, so far from helping him, gave orders for him to quit the country at once. In the end and after much bitter argument he got his timber and was permitted to make his departure. Such was the decline of Egypt that to this treatment she had no answer.

Canaan, too, was in a state of chaos. The fierce tribes east of the Jordan raided Judah and Ephraim and the Philistines were gradually becoming the masters of the land. The Hebrew tribes were in disarray and when, at Aphek, the men of Ephraim and Benjamin at last aroused themselves to confront their oppressors they were ignominiously defeated.

Bands of prophets now commenced to traverse the country and through dancing and music they attempted to re-awaken the old spirit of patriotism and unity. All that was lacking was a leader and the circumstances, as has so often occurred in history, produced the man. He was Saul, a Benjamite, the son of Kish. Saul was annointed by Samuel to be king over all Israel; the first of the Kings.

An opportunity to show his mettle soon presented itself. The Ammonites, smarting under a defeat they had recently suffered at the hand of a Hebrew, Jepthah, had encroached into Israel territory and had laid siege to Jabesh-Gilead. The inhabitants were willing to surrender, but the King of Ammon, in his terms, had demanded every man should have his right eye put out. Saul, on hearing this, cut up a yoke of oxen and sent pieces to all the tribes as a warning of what would happen to their herds if they failed to rally to him. Recognizing a leader they came forward in their thousands.

With the army which he had raised he fought a successful action against the Ammonites who were besieging Jabesh-Gilead. He next carried out campaigns against the rulers of Moab and Jobah. He marched south and settled old scores with the Edomites whose raids on Judaea, coupled with their flirtations with the Philistines, caused a constant and festering sore on Israel's southern flank.

Gratifying as these campaings were, it was the Philistines who remained his most dangerous neighbours against whom he had had two notable successes; that resulting from David's killing Goliath and that at Michmash.

By now the Philistine strategy was becoming clear; it was to secure and control the trade routes with Syria and beyond. A united Israel could mar this project and it was for this reason that the Philistines had occupied Michmash on the direct route from Ajlon to Jericho and a key position in Israel's Judah. The Plain of Esdraelon was a further zone of strategic significance through which ran the direct route to Damascus and from where they could effectively split the northern from the southern tribes of Israel.

On this background let us now examine the fatal battle that was to bring about the defeat of the Israelites and the death of Saul. Moving up the Plain of Sharon the Philistines concentrated their army at Aphek where the roads leading to the Plain of Dothan and the Pass of Megiddo bifurcate. Seeing this movement Saul concentrated his men below Mount Gilboa at Engannim from whence he could intervene if the enemy advanced eastwards or, alternatively, if they went north through Megiddo into Esdraelon he could move to the heights of Gilboa. In the event, the Philistines advanced through Megiddo and then turned eastwards to the Hills of Morah in the vicinity of Shunem. From this it was fairly clear that their objective was the River Jordan and the crossings over it; nevertheless, whatever their object, whether it was merely to occupy the rich Esdraelon Plain or to control the road to Damascus, it was obvious that Saul's army could not be permitted to remain in its commanding position on their flank. Up to this moment Saul had the initiative and the enemy must dance to his tune; the Israelite strategy seemed sound.

The problem facing the Philistines was not whether to attack Saul or not, but how to attack him. This choice was theirs and to that extent they, too, had a degree of initiative, particularly if they could do the unexpected. A direct assault from Shunem, across the open valley, over the deep stream and then up the steep slopes of Gilboa had all the disadvantages of doing the obvious, but worse than this they would be attacking over ground completely unsuited to their chariots which would cancel out one of their principal advantages. In contrast to this course the approach to the mountain from the west was over gradually rising ground with excellent going for vehicles. Here, then, if only the approach could be done with surprise, was the Achilles heel of Saul's position.

Unseen by the Israelite army the Philistines passed round Jezreel and were able to close with Saul on the gentle slopes which led up to the higher open ground where their chariots were free to manoeuvre. It was up here that they encountered the most stubborn resistance, the Israelites fighting desperately and not without hope. The battle, however, was decided when Saul received a dangerous wound from an arrow and, rather than be taken prisoner and imperious to the last, he fell upon his own sword. Jonathan also was killed as were his brothers. When the men saw that their king and princes were dead they fled.

Saul's defeat was certainly not due to any fault in his strategy or tactical design. He was in fact attacked on his one weak spot and the Philistine superiority in chariots, combined with their skilful selection of the ground on which to deploy them, won the day. Battle can sometimes turn on one incident, in this case it was the loss of the leader.

The tragedy lay not only in the sad end of a great soldier, but in the consequences of defeat. A king's life work seemed to have been shattered in one blow. The defeat of the Israelites gave the Philistines access to Esdraelon from whence they were in a position both to split the tribes and to have free access to the trade route to Syria and beyond. Not only had the Israelites lost a king, they had no obvious successor, for the king's son, Jonathan, had also been slain. But in spite of this they were about to enter possibly their greatest period; however, not without much tribulation and much hard work.

9 The campaigns of David

Saul's kingship had lasted twenty years. The extent of his successes should not be blurred by the tragedy surrounding his death; for, though he died like a hero, and to that extent paid the price of defeat in battle, he left in the minds of all his people an impression of greatness. They had tasted the sweet honey of success and they had experienced kingship of the quality they had wanted. In their hour of defeat they still had the underlying confidence that his leadership and Samuel's teaching had imparted. All they now wanted was new leadership, the leadership of a man they could implicitly trust and to whom they could give their love. This role David was ultimately to fill.

Before dealing with David's reign one should look at the long period when, through the jealousy of Saul, he was forced to lead the life of an outlaw. This was the period when, on the hard anvil of adversity, the character of a future king developed, not along lines of vindictive revenge but on the far broader basis of human understanding.

He sought refuge in the hilly country of Judaea. Here there was little water and over the stony hills one could tramp for hours feeling as solitary as at sea; yet a man might suddenly appear as though from nowhere in an area that would not seem capable of giving shelter to a rabbit. Giant squills grew along the rocks with exotic scented flowers and crocuses showed their delicate heads. In this waste David was at home. His refuge, the 'cave' of Adullam, was not far removed from his home at Bethlehem. He was joined by his family as well as by outlaws like himself. These were the men destined to be the van of his future army.

From now he led the life of a captain of guerillas, cultivating friendship with the local people who were happy to have a protector against the robbers and marauding tribesmen from Philistine and elsewhere, even if for this he demanded tribute. He foraged far and wide, bringing retribution where it was due and giving succour where it was needed. Like Robin Hood, his targets were the greedy and the wealthy, the poor he left in peace.

In Carmel in Judaea, to the south-east of Hebron, lived a wealthy fellow, a churlish man who went by the name of Nabal. David sent ten of his young men to ask for food and drink for himself and his followers. Never had they molested Nabal's shepherds nor had they stolen from him and they had protected his flocks whilst they grazed; but from Nabal they got nothing.

David decided to take by force what he had failed to get by asking. Abigail, Nabal's wife, heard of this and went out to intervene bringing with her gifts of food. When she met the outlaws she pleaded with them appealing to their chivalry. There and then David decided to let Nabal off, a decision that was not popular with his followers who, armed for the fray, were keen to get the loot which assuredly would be theirs. That his men accepted his change of front was some indication of the respect they had for David and of the discipline in which he held them. It also gives a picture of the human streak that tempered this fiery nature.

But all his exploits were not of this type. As his strength grew he harried the Amalakites and other nomad tribes that raided Judaea. His relations with the Philistines were uncertain and present a complicated picture, for he seems to have been prepared to join forces with them if it suited his book, whilst at others he marched against them. He was inevitably forced to play the hand of opportunity. When the Philistine army concentrated for its advance on Esdraelon he apparently joined them, but when recognized he was forced to flee back to his hills in Judaea. When he reached Ziklag he found the town had been plundered, his village was a ruin and all the women and their children had been taken prisoner. He called for Abiathar, who had now joined him, to bring the ephod or vestment worn by priests and, after praying, he pursued the robbers. The vigour of his pursuit soon brought him up with them and he fought them from twilight to the evening of the following day. He recovered all they had carried away, including his and his father's wives and their children, in addition to which he captured all their flocks and herds.

It was immediately after this success that he heard of the defeat of the Israelites at Gilboa and of the death of Saul and Jonathan. This ended the first and formative part of David's life; he was now thirty years of age; physically hard, experienced in war, wise and just and a fit leader of men.

After their victory the Philistines took possession of the Plain of Esdraelon and of the Vale of Jezreel. They moved into the Jordan valley and they occupied the Hills of Galilee. Cohesion between the northern tribes of Israel had gone. In spite of this, however, Saul's general, Abner, had managed to rally much of the defeated army, shattered as it had been by the disaster it had suffered and dismayed as it was by the loss of its king. He was able to concentrate the remnants of thus once bold and confident host across the Jordan near the remote city of Mahanaim, not far from Mizpah in the hilly country of Gilead.

On hearing of the disaster David went to Hebron and there he was proclaimed king of Judah. Saul's death confronted David with a problem that was as pressing as it was complex. Although the northern tribes were in disarray, he knew that loyalty to their late king and to his memory would be strong. He was determined to show by both his words and his actions how keenly he sympathized with his kinsfolk in their military disaster as well as the personal loss they had suffered. His public mourning was intended to be an indication of these feelings. His gratitude to the men of Jabesh-Gilead for their

chivalrous rescue of the bodies of Saul and his sons was prompt
and his emissaries left the people of that town in no doubt on
that score. Nevertheless, his message that, as king of Judaea he
prayed for their hands to be strengthened and for them to be
valiant, coupled with the suggestion that, perhaps, they might
look to him as a leader, fell on stony ground.

In the meantime Abner had rallied the tribes to Saul's only
surviving son, Ishbosheth, a man of mediocre character and
some ten years older than David. In tragic circumstances
Abner lost his life and without his help Ishbosheth lost hope.
Friendless and unable to stand on his own feet he was foully
murdered by two of his followers who, thinking they would
please David, brought the wretched king's head to him.
David's wrath was as unfeigned as it was intense. By act and
word he was showing himself to be a man of wisdon and understanding; nevertheless, it took a long time for him to win over
the tribes of Israel and it was not until seven years after Saul's
death that his patience won the day. All twelve tribes eventually
turned to him and at Hebron he was annointed king over all
Israel. This was one of his greatest victories.

The shepherd boy, the soldier, the outlaw, and finally the
king of Judah had now moved into the sphere of full kingship
of a great people. However he may be judged by individual
incidents in his colourful life, his greatness as a king can be
established beyond any doubt. He put first things first, and the
unity of the tribes was the first pillar of his political strategy.
He taught one of the most important lessons in political
philosophy. He set out to gain the people's confidence; but,
having gained it, he never forgot that his task was to retain it.

David had been crowned at Hebron in Judaea. He knew this
could never be the capital of Israel and that he must choose
another place, preferably on the border between Judaea and the
northern tribes. The site he selected was that of the old
Jebusite city on the high ground between the Brook Kidron and
the valley of the Kinnom, the city now called Jerusalem.
Although this was indeed an ancient town it had no particular
Hebrew affinity. At two thousand five hundred feet above sea

level it enjoyed a healthy and invigorating climate. It was a good strategic position and easily defended. The two springs at Gihon in the Kidron and the Pools of Siloam at the junction of the two rivers provided an ample water supply. It was here, immediately to the south of the old Canaanite town, that 'David's City' was erected.

Before he could build his capital the Jebusite garrison had to be overcome, and David offered the reward of commander-in-chief to the man who should achieve its capture. It was Joab who, scaling the cliffs which the Jebusites boasted were unassailable, took the city making its ruler his captive. Joab became the commander-in-chief and to his generalship must the credit for many of David's military successes go.

So long as Israel and Judah were disunited and at war and so long as both recognized their tributary status the Philistines had been content to let sleeping dogs lie; but now that the tribes were once again united they took action. They first sent a column up by the old route to Michmash, but in the Vale of Rephaim they were repulsed. Their next move was from the direction of Beth Horon on to the plateau of Gibeon, a few flat miles from Jerusalem. With his old freebooters in the van David took the initiative, again forcing them to withdraw. He pressed his advantage and success followed success. His campaign culminated in the capture of Gath and its surrounding villages. Some indication of the consequences of this war can be gauged from the fact that henceforth he had over six hundred men of Gath, men of the once dreaded Cherethite and Pelethite tribes of the Philistines, in his service and they, from now onwards, formed his personal bodyguard.

When he had settled the score with the Philistines he paid attention to his neighbours east of the Jordan, the Moabites. It was with the king of Moab that he had placed his parents at the time when he was an outlaw; betraying this trust David believed the king of Moab had had his mother and father put to death. His war against the Moabites was carried out with the greatest ferocity, two-thirds of his captives were executed and the remainder were placed under heavy tribute. He did not, however, make any attempt to incorporate Moab into his kingdom.

His next campaign, one of great significance, was forced on him by circumstances beyond his control. Relationship with Nahash, king of the Ammonites, had been extremely friendly, both during Saul's kingship and subsequent to David's election as king. When, shortly after his successful war in Moab, the king of the Ammonites died, David very naturally sent messengers to his successor, Hanun, expressing sympathy for him and hopes for continued good relations between the two kingdoms.

Unfortunately, and probably due to the reports he had received of David's treatment of the Moabites, Hanun suspected him of designs of conquest. He grossly insulted David's emissaries by cutting off their beards and, after disrobing them, he sent them back. David replied by sending an army which he placed under the command of Joab, to teach the Ammonite king a lesson in manners.

Hanun had in the meantime asked for assistance from the Aramaean states of Zoba, Beth-Rehob and Maacah which lay to the north. The Aramaean army, mustering almost thirty thousand soldiers, marched to join the Ammonites. Joab thus found himself faced by two armies and not one, and a junction between the two he realized must at all costs be prevented. The Aramaeans, who were the more numerous and the better soldiers, were to his north and threatened his rear, whilst the Ammonite army, against which he was originally deployed, lay to the east. He only had the numbers to concentrate a sufficient force against one while holding the other, and certainly could not deploy an adequate number for victory on both fronts simultaneously. Such a predicament is not unusual in war, but to extricate an army from it and to emerge victorious is rare. Joab was, in fact, forced to fight on interior lines; whilst this can have certain advantages it is equally true that a commander in this position can be open to simultaneous attack from two directions. How did Joab deal with this?

The cardinal points in his plan were as follows. First, he would adopt the offensive on one front and hold on the other;

offensive action was thus the keynote of his strategy. Second, where he intended to attack he would deploy his best troops and, of course, greater numbers. To do this he must take risks on the less important area. He must tackle the more dangerous front first and this was in the north where the Aramaeans were, for here was a threat to his lines of communication to Israel. Were he to attack the Ammonites first and, even if this was successful, he would, after being inevitably weakened, forced to face an army standing between him and his own country, and would then have to fight a battle on ground of the enemy's choosing.

These factors decided him. He picked his best men and deployed them for attack against the Aramaeans, whilst to his brother, Abishai, he allotted the task of containing the Ammonites. Nevertheless, he was not satisfied with this alone. He had to think of the contingency of the Aramaeans proving too strong for him and in this event Abishai was, therefore, to be prepared to move over to support him. In the event his attack on the Aramaeans was successful and their army fled before him.

With this threat liquidated and his lines of communication now secure he hastened to the assistance of his brother. Seeing themselves hopelessly outnumbered the Ammonites withdrew to the cover of their city, Rabbah-Ammon, where they prepared for siege. Joab invested the city and, when he had brought matters so far that the place was about to fall, he summoned David that he might enjoy the honour of making the capture himself.

Ammon was no longer troublesome and David's treatment of the people was far less severe than that which he had meted out to the Moabites. The prisoners he took were, however, set to labour with saws, axes and brickmoulds for the work on the royal projects in the city of David. Ammon, like Moab, was made to pay tribute, but the land was left under the rule of its native prince.

The Aramaean menace had, however, only been temporarily disposed of. Habadezar, who held hegemony over the

Aramaean peoples at this time, called the tribes together and placed them under the command of his general, Shobach. David despatched the whole Israelite army against the coalition. After re-crossing the Jordan, Joab moved north and encountered the enemy near Halom, which lay in the descent from the highlands about Ijon to the west of Mount Hermon. The battle that ensued had far-reaching consequences, for it resulted in a complete victory for Joab, the Israelites slaying the men of several hundred chariots as well as many thousand horsemen. Shobach, their general, fell in the combat. The victory over the Aramaeans was followed by the capture of Damascus and an advance as far as the Upper Euphrates. The Aramaeans, who earlier had been sufficiently powerful to initiate a campaign for the conquest of Assyria, were henceforth to pay tribute to Israel. David's kingdom now extended from the Euphrates to the Mediterranean and as far north as Kadesh.

The Israelite's next war was against the kingdom of the Edomites. When the Edomites were friendly, the Hebrews had enjoyed the fruits of their commerce, for they were so placed that the trade between Egypt and the north as well as with the Arab world passed through Edomite territories, which were also astride the important road east of the Jordan through Moab and Ammon to Damascus. However, when the Edomites decided to ally themselves with the Philistines and the tribes of Moab, they embarked on a vicious series of attacks on the Hebrews and their trade with the peoples of Arabia and Egypt. The Edomites raided deep into Judah and had in recent years carried off hundreds of prisoners. Some of these had been sold as slaves to Philistines in Gaza and others to Phoenicians in Tyre. The descendants of Esau, were a hot-headed and virile people. David concluded that complete subjugation and annexation of their territory was the only practical cure for this festering sore.

The conduct of operations was placed in the capable hands of Joab. After an easily gained success in the Valley of Salt between Beersheba and the Dead Sea he invaded Edom, ravaging the land and putting to the sword every man who fell into his hands. Edom, unlike Moab and Ammon, was not allowed to retain its own government and, losing all independence, was annexed to Judah, and was fully garrisoned by Israelite troops. Their king perished in the war, but his little son, Hadad, escaped to Egypt, later to reappear as a formidable antagonist to Solomon.

David was wise enough not to quarrel with the Phoenicians, who occupied all the long coastal territories to the north of Mount Carmel. The Phoenicians were both powerful and wealthy. David, in later years, concluded arrangements with their king, Hiram, by which he was supplied with cedar wood for the building of his city. From Hiram, he also obtained masons and skilled carpenters for the construction of his palace, for the Phoenicians had lost nothing of the skills that had so characterized their work during the Amana period, skills the Israelites certainly did not at this time possess. Hiram, who was younger than David, lived for many years and well into the period of Solomon's reign. He was a man of peace and his rule marked one of the most prosperous eras in Phoenician history.

With Ammon, Moab and the Aramaean kingdoms all tributary, with Edom incorporated into Judah and Phoenicia friendly, David was now ruling a very powerful state.

One must remark here on his exercise of kingship. An erstwhile leader of outlaws, a born fighter and a soldier at heart, one would have expected him to lead his armies personally in the field, and this certainly would have been consonant with the custom of the times. But the king of Israel had other views. He thought in terms of his kingdom as a whole and this demanded his guidance and a firm grip of government. This strength of mind which enabled him to direct his wars from his capital, leaving the conduct of his campaigns to his generals, played no small part in his success as a monarch. It enabled him to keep a hold on his own countrymen and to preserve the home front in what was a new state. His combination of martial genius and administrative leadership are rare qualities; the bonds that held the Israelites and the men of Judah together were new and at best fragile.

As so frequently happens in the affairs of nations, those internal differences, which are forgotten in moments of fear, once the outside threat of hostile invasion is removed, are too soon in evidence again. If any dissensions were to manifest themselves in the kingdom, they would develop in the northern territories among the tribes of which the old loyalties to Saul and the almost traditional jealousy of Judah would provide the media for the revolutionary activities of pretenders or would-be usurpers.

As oriental kings aged and their sons grew older the eyes of the place-seekers naturally turned to the most probable successor. It was normal, too, for the son who aspired to succession to do all in his power to establish his position. Absalom, David's eldest son, was no exception. His revolt against his father makes sad reading, as do the vacillations of the courtiers and the intrigues to which they stooped. At this stage old Joab stands out as a loyal, forthright and vigorous lieutenant. To the king one would expect the men of Judah to be loyal as would be the Philistine mercenaries and the Cherizite bodyguard. When Absalom revolted he and those Israelites who supported him were signally defeated in the woods of Ephraim by Joab's skill, and in the fight Absalom was killed. David's remorse, which was displayed publicly, was deep and sincere.

However, to Joab it was obvious that the king's grief, understandable as it was, might be construed by those who had been loyal and who had stood by him as a repudiation. He warned the king that unless he showed his gratitude to those who had risked all for him 'there would not tarry one with thee this night.' Joab, a wise counsellor, a loyal friend and a capable soldier, shows up at this time in all the welter of place-seeking, snivelling and miserable courtiers as a pillar of strength. It was unquestionably due to him that David was able to squash the rebellion, although at the cost of the loss of his favourite son, and eventually to pass on to his successor a united kingdom.

Saul at his death left Israel defeated and humiliated. David raised the people from these depths to a state of great prosperity, a prosperity in which the people shared; and, by his successful campaigns and conquests, he made the hitherto small and comparatively unimportant confederation of Hebrew tribes one of the most powerful and respected states in the Near East.

In summing up his character we find that, of all things, he was human; he understood his fellow men and it was this that enabled him to exert such a powerful influence over Israel. In the end we are left with an unqualified admiration for a character that was strong in adversity, steady in success, spiritually humble, and loving and warm in its affections. That he suffered when he fell to temptation we know; but we also know that when greatness was demanded of him he could and did rise to the finest heights. His old age was not easy; yet he died loyal to his beliefs, loyal to his promises, loyal to Bathsheba and her son, Solomon; and he left the kingdom that he had created wealthy, powerful and respected.

10 The decline and fall of David's kingdom

The rift that was to cause the collapse of David's kingdom commenced with the quarrel between Rehoboam and Jeroboam. Immediately on his father's death Solomon's son, Rehoboam, went to Shechem where the tribes had foregathered to elect him king. The air was charged. What manner of king would Rehoboam make? Would he continue with the extravagant and oppressive habits of his father? Would he reduce the burden of taxation? Would he return to the simple way of life or would he continue the costly court that had made his father so unpopular in his later years?

At the same time Jeroboam, who had fled from Solomon to Egypt, returned, not as a revolutionary but as a loyal leader of a powerful section of the community, and fully prepared to co-operate, provided Rehoboam was sensible. The choice the latter had to make was simple. Was he to be stiff-necked and arrogant or was he to be conciliatory? His older advisers advocated conciliation, but the younger men wanted the tough line. A tough policy in certain circumstances may pay, in others it simply creates resistance and this can turn into revolution. Rehoboam decided to take the advice of the younger people.

Now, and not until now, did Jeroboam show his hand. The men of Israel rallied to him and only Judah stood by Rehoboam, who wanted to attack Israel at once; but in this the elders refused to support him and his army melted away. This rift was to deepen and the stage to be set for a tragedy, the extent of which could never have been foreseen by those who brought it about.

The weakness of the Hebrews, now divided among themselves, did not go unnoticed in Egypt. The pharaoh, Sheshonk, had given asylum to Jeroboam and so, hearing of the latter's defection and of the separation into two kingdoms, he seized the opportunity to stake his claims on the divided land. In the fifth year of Rehoboam's reign he invaded Canaan with a powerful and well-organized army. He was everywhere successful, he siezed Esdraelon and marched into the Vale of Jezreel, even crossing the Jordan, an area that had not seen Egyptian troops for over two hundred years. He let loose his Libyan mercenaries who plundered from Rehob at the Source of the Jordan to Beersheba in the south, pillaging towns and destroying villages. Entering Jerusalem the Libyans despoiled it of the wealth it had accumulated in David's and Solomon's reigns. From Sheshonk's records it is clear that his campaign was directed impartially against both kingdoms and not against Israel alone. The Egyptian treasury was replenished with the plunder they took; however, not content with this, they placed the whole country under tribute. They put a governor over the Sinai and the caravan route to the east.

The kings of Israel and Judah who followed were poor and ineffectual, and not until the arrival of Omri in 885 did any leave a mark. This remarkable man came to power as a result of a *coup d'état*. Elah, king of Israel, while carousing with his chamberlain in Tirzah, the then capital, was assassinated by Zimri who thereupon seized the throne; but the army, which at that time was beseiging the Philistines at Gibbethon, refused to recognize him and proclaimed Omri, their general, as king.

Omir was a military and political organizer of first rank. He raised the kingdom of Israel from a position of obscurity to one of considerable influence in Canaan and beyond. The fame of Omir spread far and wide; as far, even, as Assyria where he was held in such esteem that Israel was known as the Land of Omri; years after he and his dynasty had fallen it continued to bear his name and the kings of Israel were called the sons of Omri. His principal achievements were that he united the northern tribes; he formed an alliance with Ethbaal, king of Tyre, thus cementing an old friendship; he settled scores with the Moabites from whom he received tribute; and he kept the peace with Judah.

His alliance with Tyre was important because it enabled the two countries of Phoenicia and Israel to show a united front to Assyria whose ambitions were always a threat to their security. They were together able to control the trade routes from the Euphrates to the Mediterranean ports.

Having settled his relations with Phoenicia he next turned his attention to Moab. He invaded the country as since the division of the two Hebrew kingdoms the Moabites had ceased payment of the tribute David had exacted. In Moab he built cities at Ataroth and Jahaz. From the spoils of his Moabite ventures he bought the site for and built the city of Samaria.

Samaria, a name so significant from now onwards in the history of Canaan, was built some six miles from Shechem in a well-watered valley which here opened into a wide basin. The actual site was upon the level top of an oblong hill with accessible though steep sides, and known then as the Hill of Shemer, the name of its owner and from whom it was bought. Omri's vision in selecting this site has been likened to that of Constantine when he fixed Constantinople as his capital.

From Samaria one had a full view of the hills around Shechem to the south and of Ebal and Gerizim to the east, while across the Plain of Sharon to the west could be seen the deep blue waters of the Mediterranean. Although Omri gave it the name of Samaria, in Assyria it was called Beth Kumri, the Palace of Omri.

Omri never succeeded in dominating the Aramaean capital at Damascus and its king, Ben Hadad, in fact obtained concessions which included an area in the new capital city for the merchants of Damascus. The interest in this lay in the indication it gives of Omri's willingness to compromise; he seemed to possess the invaluable gift of knowing when to fight and when to negotiate; with whom to fight and for how long; and with whom to make peace. As an example of this he kept the peace with the king of Judah, which enabled him to deal with his other projects unhampered by fear of interference from his southern neighbours.

Omri died in the year 874 leaving Israel strong in her alliance with Tyre and well placed in regard to Damascus. He had subdued Moab and was at peace with Judah. In religious matters he was indifferent and married his son to Jezebal, a notorious follower of Astarte, a union which was to have tragic consequences. Omri had been a man of the sword, a successful general and a capable negotiator.

He was succeeded by his son Ahab, a worthless man. Ahab quarrelled with Judah against which he commenced warlike operations. The latter was, however, in a sad state of decline and was little more than a vassal of Israel—paying tribute and only when required providing soldiers. Some indication of this decline can be gauged from the fact that in none of the annals of the Assyrian kings of this period are Judah or Judaea even mentioned.

Truly David's kingdom had collapsed.

11 The end of Israel and the fall of Jerusalem

In a short space of two hundred years Israel ceased to exist and its people were compulsorily removed to be replaced by foreign immigrants; Judaea was twice overrun, Jerusalem sacked and the population taken captive to Babylon. Assyria first dominated the scene; but later it was Babylon.

In 747, about a hundred years after Omri's death, Tiglath-Pileser III came to the throne at Nineveh. This second Assyrian Empire differed from its predecessor in the political concept of its king, which was based not on conquest for conquest's sake, but on an attempt to concentrate on a hegemony of bureaucratic nature in which each country paid a fixed tax and provided a stated military contigent. The Assyrian campaigns were, thus, more than raids to plunder; they had a definite objective which was simply to divert trade and wealth into the royal treasury. It was with this ambitious end in view that Tiglath-Pileser overran Armenia and the hitherto strong kingdom of Damascus, and this was why he broke the power of the Hittites and then seized the Phoenician seaports and, on the Euphrates made himself master of Babylon.

His ideas for the organization of his army were also new. The army he built up was not raised on the customary 'ad hoc' basis, but was a regular professional standing army having a code of military discipline. It had its infantry and archers, but in its composition it differed from the others in that its element for mobility was provided by horsemen instead of chariots. It was these wild Assyrian cavalrymen who, swarming round the flanks, were to strike terror into the hearts of their enemy. This was something new in warfare, and in war it is the new that surprises and gives all the elements required for success.

The two Hebrew kingdoms were at war and Israel, allied to Damascus, had actually laid siege to Jerusalem. Ahaz, the king of Judah, sent a message of appeal for help to Nineveh which the king was only too happy to acknowledge. In the campaign that followed Syria was defeated and Damascus fell. Tiglath-Pileser held court in the old city where all were called to pay their homage and Ahaz, as a vassal, bowed the knee. He had, however, through his voluntary submission saved Jerusalem and his land.

In 739 Tiglath-Pileser III died. The degree of confusion that set in at the Assyrian capital gave Syria and Israel the opportunity to revolt. However, the new king, Shalmaneser, soon settled matters at his capital and returned to Damascus and Phoenicia. After restoring order here and putting down a revolt in Cyprus he marched south to deal with Israel. He laid siege to Samaria, but while this was in progress he died. The throne was seized by a usurper, Sargon, who continued the siege and within a year, three years after it had started, the city fell. Twenty-seven thousand Israelites were deported and settled in Media, their places being filled by immigrants from Babylonia. Israel became a province of Assyria and Samaria, its once proud capital, the residence of the Assyrian governor. Meanwhile Judah, though paying tribute, remained unmolested.

When Sargon died in 705 he was succeeded by his son, Sennacherib, a vain and pompous man, who possessed neither the political sagacity nor the military genius of his father. Egged on by Egypt, Hezekiah, the king of Judah, decided to revolt. This brought a haughty ultimatum from Sennacherib in which he recalled that Assyrian armies had destroyed all the surrounding lands both this side and east of the Jordan; he then laid siege to Jerusalem which, however, he was unable to take.

As a fortress city Jerusalem possessed certain natural advan-

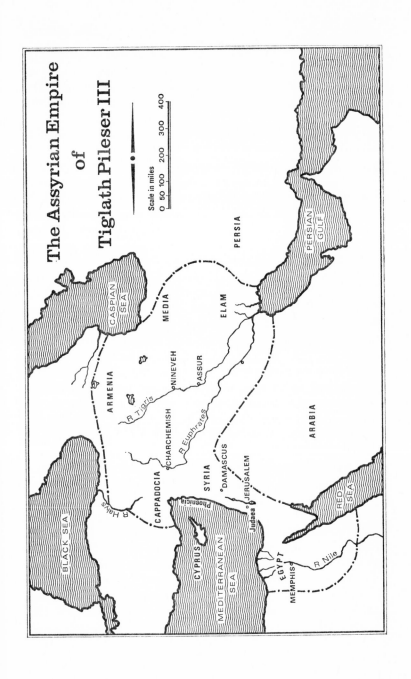

The Assyrian Empire
of
Tiglath Pileser III

Scale in miles
0 50 100   200   300   400

CASPIAN
SEA

MEDIA

PERSIA

ARMENIA

NINEVEH

ASSUR

ELAM

R Tigris

PERSIAN
GULF

CHARCHEMISH

R Euphrates

CAPPADOCIA

ARABIA

BLACK SEA

R Halys

SYRIA

°DAMASCUS

°JERUSALEM

Judaea°

Phoenicia

CYPRUS

MEDITERRANEAN
SEA

RED
SEA

EGYPT

R Nile

MEMPHIS°

tages. It stood forbiddingly on a rocky plateau which projected southwards from a long ridge of bare hills. On the east the deep revine of the Kidron lay between it and the Mount of Olives, while on the south and west it was protected by the valley of the Hinnom. Both valleys dropped steeply to their point of junction which was several hundred feet below the general level of the plateau. With its strong, thick and high walls, and the natural advantages of its position, it was an easy city to defend. Furthermore, its water supply was good.

When, therefore, Sennacherib commenced his siege he was undertaking no small enterprise.

The Assyrian armies when fighting in the open had defeated their enemies by their superior discipline, the mobility which their cavalry gave them and, finally, by their superior numbers. However, when it came to attacking walled cities they did not seem to possess either the armament or the skills necessary for this type of warfare. They relied, instead, on the slow process of starving the defenders to a point of submission. Samaria held out for three years and Jerusalem looked like doing the same. But, while the siege was at its height, the Assyrian army was decimated by plague and sadly depleted was forced to withdraw to Nineveh.

By now the long drawn out efforts to maintain order in her far-flung possessions inevitably began to tell on Assyria's diminishing wealth and fighting man-power. She was throughout this period harassed by Scythian hordes whom she was unable to contain.

It was the combination of these circumstances that encouraged Egypt to attempt to regain something of her lost prestige in Syria and Canaan. This policy was first pursued by Psamtek I who succeeded in so improving his country's overall position that when, in 609, he was succeeded by his son, Necho, Egypt was well balanced to take more militant action. Necho first built a fleet and with it landed troops in Philistia at Gaza and Askalon, neither of which towns offered much resistance. He now collected and equipped a large army with which he marched up through Canaan to do battle with the Assyrians.

Josiah, the young king of Judah, in the face of the advice of his ministers, decided to attack the Egyptian army. In a short engagement at Megiddo he was routed and, wounded on the battlefield, was carried to Jerusalem where he died.

Necho pressed on to the Euphrates, but Assyria was by now so near her end that she did not put up even the semblance of a resistance; in fact Necho found no army to fight. Rather strangely he did not advance on the capital at Nineveh, but rested content with consolidating his gains, which in any circumstances were considerable. Indeed, at one stroke and with little loss, he had regained the whole of the old Asian empire of Egypt. He returned to Canaan and camped at Riblah on the banks of the Orontes exactly three months after the defeat of Josiah at Megiddo.

While all this was in progress the final break-up of Assyria was drawing to its inevitable end. The kings of Babylon and Media had come to an agreement and had for some time been acting in concert. In less than two years their combined armies had completed the defeat of their fast decaying neighbour; the city of Nineveh was taken and sacked. The two victorious powers them agreed to divide the conquered territories between them, Babylon taking all to the south and west and Media all to the east.

To establish her position Babylon first had to deal with Egypt. Nabopolassar, king of Babylon, was a man well advanced in years and so he sent his son, Nebuchadrezzar, in command of the army to accomplish this task.

At a battle fought at Carchemish on the Euphrates, a battle that for Canaan had the most profound consequences, the Egyptians were utterly routed. Necho's defeat here and his subsequent conduct show that he was a man with feet of clay. His power and his will to resist were so broken that he made no attempt to stand anywhere. His army, retreating ignominiously and in a complete state of disorder, was pursued relentlessly by Nebuchadrezzar. The rout of this once boastful army as it hurried through Canaan had a deep effect on the prophet

Jeremiah, who succinctly remarked that the king of Egypt was but a noise that had passed its appointed time.

Nebuchadrezzar's father died and he had to return to the capital and this, and this alone, saved Egypt from further humiliation. Nevertheless, before he left he came to an understanding with Necho that the whole Syro-Canaan area was in future to be recognized as being part of the Babylonian domain.

Necho's defeat and this agreement should have killed any pretensions Egypt might nourish concerning her influence in this area; but it was not so. As soon as Nebuchadrezzar had departed Egypt tried to stir up trouble in Canaan, promising support to their people if they revolted. Lured by these blandishments Judah began to think herself strong enough to defy Babylon, but as soon as he had settled matters at home Nebuchadrezzar returned. The king of Judah, realizing that the expected help from Egypt was not going to materialize, cast himself on the mercy of the Babylonian. His life was spared; nevertheless he was taken prisoner and his mother, his sons and all his officers were all incarcerated with him. Ten thousand soldiers and many hundreds of craftsmen were also deported. Mattaniah, a young man of twenty, was made governor of the province which now came direct under Babylonian rule.

The third, final and tragic phase of this war now unfolded itself. Nebuchadrezzar had been forced to raise the siege of Tyre, which he had just undertaken, in order to return to his country to deal with his old enemies, the Elamites. Syria saw in this an opportunity to regain some of her lost prestige and, with the encouragement of Egypt, she formed a confederation to oppose Babylon. To Jerusalem came emissaries from Tyre and Sidon, from Ammon, Moab and Edom, all pressing her to join the revolt. Egypt now took a more prominent part, telling the king of Judah that with her army she would support him if he revolted. Judah listened and repudiated her solemn obligations with Babylon. This marked the end.

Nebuchadrezzar marched into Judaea with his divisions of cavalry, chariots and infantry accompanied by their engineers and siege weapons. Conquering city after city and breaking down resistance they were soon left with but three strongholds to suppress, the fortresses of Azekah and Lachish in the south and the capital city of Jerusalem.

Azekah had been strongly built on the slopes of a hill some thousand feet above sea level overlooking the Vale of Elah, from where one could see over across the cultivated fields and olive groves of Philistia and on to the blue Mediterranean beyond. Lachish was further to the south and lay in the middle of the coastal plain to the north-east of Gaza.

Nebuchadrezzar first attacked Azekah which eventually fell. Through relay stations the two fortresses were in touch with one another and only when signals from Azekah ceased did Joash, the commander at Lachish, know that the place had been captured. The fortress at Lachish stood on an isolated hill and was strong having double walls and a triple gate. The siege is of interest not only on account of the bravery of the defenders but for the methods of forcing a breach which the Babylonians adopted. The fortress had successfully withstood a siege by the Assyrians and so confidence was high. What they did not expect was the way in which their walls were to be overcome. Past masters at all forms of incendiarism their engineers used heat to burst open the walls. Every tree and everything that would burn was plied up against the walls and set alight; day in and day out the flames were fed until the heat grew unbearable. More and more fuel was piled on until eventually the stones, now white with heat, burst out and the walls collapsed.

With these two fortresses liquidated Nebuchadrezzar now marched on Jerusalem to which he laid siege. Surrounding the city he was content to starve it out, and the grim long drawn out operation commencing on the tenth day of the tenth month in the year 587 culminated in the fall of the city a year later. The people looked for the promised intervention by the Egyptian army, but were doomed to disappointment, for of help they got none.

Pestilence, illness and desertions added to the horrors of the siege. When the city fell the temple, the palace and all the principal buildings were razed to the ground and the rest was burned. All the priests were put to death. In view of the strength of the walls it would seem that treachery played its part in this affair; the walls of a fortress can be as indestructible as man can make them, but their strength ultimately lies in the will of the defenders and, not least, on their loyalty.

This was the high water mark of Babylonian power. Within fifty years Babylon was destroyed and Semitic influence commenced to decay. Syria had been already eclipsed and Assyria had ceased to exist; now Babylon was about to fall. In Canaan neither the Philistines nor the Phoenicians were any longer of consequence, and the Hebrew community was in disarray. The great Semitic race was without leadership and entered on a period of decline which, with one exception, was to last a thousand years.

12 The military achievements of Persia

Against a background of Semitic decay the kingdom of Cyrus was born and, under his successors, flourished. It included Media, Babylonia and all the lands of the Fertile Crescent, as well as Egypt, Thrace and Macedonia; in the east, Persian conquests spread as far as Baluchistan and the lands watered by the Oxus and the Indus. Kashmir and the Pamirs also bowed to their rule.

The rise of Persia was phenomenal.

Who were the Persians? The name in origin strictly denoted the district known as Parsis and the word Persian applied primarily to those people who lived in that area. Custom has, however, extended the name to all those who dwelt on the Iranian plateau. In this story I employ the word Persian as this is used so much in biblical and contemporary writings. The Persians were of 'Aryan' stock of which word the name Iran is, in fact, a variant. The original Persians came from the great steppes stretching from north of the Black Sea and the Caspian through South Russia. From these regions they gradually penetrated south, one part spreading into India across the Indus and on to the Gangetic Plain, while the other moved west to the borders of the Semitic world.

As with all early civilizations the character of Persian religion underwent periodic changes, but the most far-reaching of these occurred with the teachings of the philosopher,

Zoroaster. His thesis was that in the world there were two groupings of power, the one for good and the other for evil. He saw light as a symbol against evil, with which he associated darkness and destruction. Riding between the opposites of good and evil man is placed, free to choose. The man-made gods of vulgar belief he discarded and the basis of his philosophy was purely abstract and the abstractions which he preached were the ethical forces which dominated human life. He saw his religion as unrestricted by any form of national barrier and from the first it aimed at propaganda. It was the first creed to work by mission and to lay claims to universal acceptance.

This background of racial origin and of religious influence gives the clue to the liberal form of government, the understanding, and the sympathetic treatment of captured people, that characterized Cyrus and his immediate successors.

Cyrus, founder of the Persian Empire, was born of Achaemenid stock and, although he lived in Elam, he was certainly not an Elamite. Both he and his father were devout Zoroastrians.

He succeeded his father in 558 and five years later led a successful rebellion against the Medes whose vassal the king of Anshan was. In this revolt he was supported by some of the more important Persian tribes and, after his initial success, the remaining people willingly acknowledged him as their leader. From this point onward he styled himself as king of Persia. At first Nabonidus, king of Babylon, hailed the fall of the Medes, but it was not long before he saw the dangers that would result from the new position. He, therefore, formed an alliance with Egypt, Lydia and Sparta and, with his new-found friends, attacked Cyrus. The Persians, at a bloody battle in Cappadocia, routed the coalition. By 546 Cyrus's armies had reached the shores of the Mediterranean and, in the following year, he had forced the majority of the Greek ports in Asia Minor to surrender, while Cilicia had acknowledged his suzerainty. In 539 he formally occupied Babylon and in the east he embarked on a campaign of conquests which included Baluchistan and India as far as the River Indus. In the space of twenty-five years he established an empire on enlightened lines in which the Persian masters were both liked and respected.

Cyrus had the ability to confirm his military successes by adopting a liberal form of government for the vanquished. There was nothing mean or paltry in his concepts. He respected the feelings of the people over whom he ruled. As an example, we find that the whole population, whether Persian or conquered, were liable to the same military service. Within the Satrapies into which he divided his territories, subject races were given the greatest freedom and were, to a surprisingly tolerant degree, independent. In Judaea the Hebrews were permitted to convene their own popular assembly of elders and priests. Judaea with Samaria, Ashdod and the rest of the land west of the Jordan and the island of Cyprus formed the 5th Satrapy.

Cyrus issued a proclamation to the Hebrews in exile which was as inspired as it was historically important. In this he charged them to rebuild the temple at Jerusalem for which work he freed them to return, and those who did not wish to go were to help with their wealth.

On his death Cyrus was succeeded by his son, Cambyses, who turned his attention to Egypt which in 525 he invaded. Egypt's Greek allies with the fleet defected to the Persians and, in a decision battle at Pelusium, the Egyptians were defeated and their capital Memphis capitulated. The Pharaoh, Psamtek III, after leading an abortive revolt, was executed and a Persian dynasty from this time ruled in the Nile Valley for nearly two hundred years.

For the Persian outstanding military achievements we must look primarily to their tactical concepts and method of fighting. That these ultimately failed against the Greeks is no argument against the validity of the Persian concepts, rather was it due to the tendency of the Persians to adhere to a tactical idea when the circumstances were different: One must adjust tactics to changing conditions, and this ultimately the Persians failed to do. What were these Persian tactics? In what manner did they differ from those of their opponents?

The Egyptians, the Assyrians and the Babylonians had all placed great confidence on in-fighting, the man with the spear or lance protecting himself with a strong shield. The chariot and horsemen also played an important part and, when used on suitable ground in large numbers, the enemy ranks were penetrated and confusion turned to rout. Though the bow and arrow were extensively employed (particularly had the Egyptians exploited this weapon in their naval action against the Philistines) the full utilization of the weapon was never the corner-stone of their tactics.

In the Persian army of Cyrus the infantryman armed with the bow and arrow formed the '*arme blanche*,' to whom everything else was ancillary. Though their soldiers carried short lances and daggers, it was not by these weapons nor by hand-to-hand combate that tactical victory was sought. The central theme was that of overwhelming the enemy with a hail of arrows and never permitting him to come to close quarters. Their cavalry, for which they were justly famed, swarmed round the hostile flanks, throwing the foe into confusion and exploiting the discomfiture caused by the fire of the archers. Persian tactics did not merely pay lip-service to fire power; they made it the foundation of their tactical thought. Another important point was that their archers were not borne down by the weight of heavy defensive shields and armour. They had to be mobile, capable of rapid movement to meet the changing circumstances of the battle. Nevertheless, their defensive power if their lines should be broken was weak, and this proved to be their Achilles' heel when they came up against the fierce onslaughts of the Greeks and Spartans at Plataea.

This campaign, which resulted in the defeat of an army and the almost total loss of the Persian fleet, was undertaken by Xerxes with the object of putting a stop to Greek interference in Asia Minor. It met with initial success, the Greek fleet was defeated, Athens was taken and the Greek army was driven back to its last line of defence on the Isthmus of Corinth while her fleet was apparently sealed off in the Bay of Salamis.

After this why were the Persians defeated and what were the causes of their reverses?

Xerxes's strategy was based on a combination of sea and land power. His army in the Peloponnese was depending on reinforcements which were carried in the fleet. When, with the loss of over six thousand soldiers who had to be abandoned on shore, this fleet was destroyed, the scales had turned.

Nevertheless, on the field of Marathon the Persians faced a Greek army which was on the defensive. At first neither side was willing to attack, but the Persians eventually took the initiative. Their tactics were based on the action of cavalry which, charging the Greek lines, at short range threw their javelins and shot their arrows, wheeling away without coming to close quarters. To these tactics the Greeks, who suffered heavy casualties, had no answer.

Though by nightfall their lines were still intact their position was precarious and so, under cover of darkness, they withdrew to Plataea to join up with the Spartan infantry. The move was clumsily carried out and was not completed by dawn. With daylight the Persians renewed their attack. It was at this point that the Spartans intervened. Their infantry, moving in the massed phalanx adopted by the Greeks, penetrated the Persian ranks which, suffering heavily, were forced to withdraw ignominiously to their camp. The Athenians and Spartans had won the day. Persian cavalry were not even used, for neither the ground nor the circumstances of the battle were favourable to them.

The causes of Persia's defeat were fourfold. First, the loss of her fleet and her consequent inability to protect her sea lines of communication was a major contributory cause; second, the weakness of her tactical system in battle when her troops were thrown on the defensive; third, her army in Greece consisted largely of levies found from all over the empire and it was these levies that gave way before the Spartan attacks; finally, the fighting stamina of the Spartans and the effectiveness of their hoplites was too much for her exhausted soldiers who missed the Persian reinforcements that had been put ashore at the time of the disastrous fleet action.

For Persia this was a serious reverse. The Greeks, pressing their advantage, attempted to seize Cyprus and to obtain a footing in the Nile Delta, but in neither of these enterprises were they successful. By the Peace of Callias, signed thirty years after the Battle of Plataea, the Greeks were forced to renounce all war-like operations against the Persians and had to be content with the latter's promises not to attack Greek possessions. This uneasy peace did not last for long.

13 The campaigns of Alexander

Internecine strife between the Greeks made them an easy prey to renewed pressure from the decaying Persians under Artaxerxes III. Although Persia was the common enemy, even against her, the Greeks were disunited and, fiercely autonomous, they lacked both cohesion and centralized control. These, however, were now unexpectedly to come from Macedon.

When, in 359, Philip became king of that country, more for his own security than for anything else, he carried out a series of campaigns against the Greek states which, culminating in the battle of Chaeroneia, resulted in his being the virtual head of all the Greeks. This position they now accepted and, with a view to regaining what they had lost to the Persians in the following year they unanimously voted him for their projected war Captain-General of all Hellenic forces. Before he had completed arrangements for this he was assassinated.

As king of Macedon he was succeeded by his son, Alexander, who at the Diet of Corinth was elected as Hellenic Captain-General in his father's place. Educated by Aristotle, he had been brought up to venerate Greek culture which was to influence him in the political decisions he subsequently had to make. He was a man possessed of an intensely strong ambition, perhaps he was the most ambitious man of history.

The heights to which this ambition soared soon became apparent. Whereas the intentions of his father had been limited to wresting Greek possessions from Persian control, Alexander's aim was nothing less than the annihilation of the Persian Empire. He intended to conquer the world and to establish the Hellenic way of life in all the countries he conquered. The indelible mark he made on history is due to this latter aim, and not merely to his military successes, great as these were. Success for success's sake meant nothing to him. neither did empire. It was the spread of Hellenic culture which was the mainspring of all he undertook.

As a soldier he was methodical and essentially practical. He first made sure of his position in Macedonia and in the Greek states and when, and only when he was satisfied that all was well on the home front did he set out on his campaigns. Two years after his father's death he crossed the Hellespont with an army of between thirty and forty thousand men.

With the immediate threat of attack from Darius III at the head of a Persian army in the Granicus, and with his only communication to his base being across the Hellespont and with the Persian fleet at large, Alexander had little scope for initiative. Undoubtedly Persian strategy should have been to draw him well inland and then to have attacked his rear with the object of severing his sensitive lines of communication; but the Persians decided to go forward and fight.

During the battle that ensued the contest was bitter; but the splendid Greek infantry were too strong for the Persians whose lightly armed men were incapable of standing up against the massed attacks of the Greek hoplites, and the latter, in their solid formations were able to withstand the charges of Persian cavalry. The lessons of Plataea had not been absorbed and Darius was inexorably forced to give way. By nightfall his once confident army was in full retreat leaving the road through Anatolia completely open.

With a view to the following year's operations Alexander now concentrated his army at Gordium, an important meeting-place of roads in northern Phrygia. It was here that, with one stroke of his sword, he cut the famous Gordian knot of cornel bark that bound the yoke of the pole of the car in which King

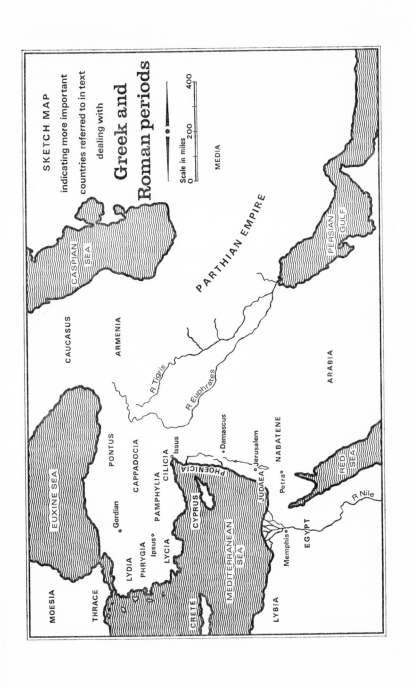

SKETCH MAP
indicating more important
countries referred to in text
dealing with

Greek and
Roman periods

Scale in miles
0   200   400

MEDIA

PARTHIAN EMPIRE

CASPIAN
SEA

CAUCASUS

ARMENIA

R. Tigris

R. Euphrates

PERSIAN
GULF

ARABIA

EUXINE SEA

PONTUS

LYDIA

PHRYGIA

Gordian

Ipsus

CAPPADOCIA

PAMPHYLIA

LYCIA

CILICIA

Issus

Damascus

PHOENICIA

Jerusalem

JUDAEA

Petra

NABATENE

RED
SEA

R. Nile

EGYPT

Memphis

LYBIA

MEDITERRANEAN
SEA

CYPRUS

CRETE

THRACE

MOESIA

Gordius rode to the temple of Zeus. The oracle said that whoever succeeded in cutting this strong entwined knot should reign over all Asia.

Though freshly organized Greek squadrons were making their presence felt in the Mediterranean this was not enough, and not until he had succeeded in closing all ports to the Persian fleet could Alexander feel secure. The capture and closure of these ports was, therefore, the next aim of his strategy. This involved risks and by concentrating on the ports and leaving his eastern flank open he was taking a big chance, a chance Darius was quick to seize. He now struck at Alexander's lines of communication through Anatolia, a strategy he might with great advantage have adopted earlier. To do this now Darius had to move his army through intricate mountainous country and the temporary disadvantage in which this placed him Alexander was able to see. Turning his army round he attacked the Persians while their forces were split and, at Issus, he inflicted on them a second and far more serious defeat. However, he did not press the pursuit, for his main objective still remained the closure of the ports. With the Persian army no longer a serious factor he was able to undertake these operations without fear of interruption. Darius had sued for peace and was prepared to accord all his possessions in Syria, Canaan and Egypt to Alexander. But to the Macedonian there was no alternative to complete surrender. The scope of his grand design was becoming clear.

On the Levant there were two ports of significance, the first was Tyre and the second Gaza. Both resisted stubbornly; but in turn each fell. The Phoenician city of Tyre was a combination of skilfully designed heavy fortifications and natural strength. It was built on a small island in close proximity to the coastline. The Greeks had two difficulties to overcome. The first was to get the assault towers close enough to the walls of the fortress to be effective, and the second was to construct towers of sufficient height and strength for the task.

To deal with the first problem Alexander constructed a mole six hundred and fifty yards in length from the coastline to the walls of the fort. These operations were continuously hindered by a hail of missiles which the defenders hurled on the heads of the engineers. However, by using their shields as cover the Greeks eventually succeeded in completing this task.

In order to be able to fire down on the defence the assault towers had to be built to a height of some hundred and sixty feet. These were constructed on the mainland and eventually moved up into position by prodigious efforts on the part of the engineers. Once these 'helepoleis,' as they were termed, were in position, a drawbridge, cunningly placed at the top, enabled the Greeks to deliver an effective surprise attack. The towers were twenty storeys high. The preparations for all this immense work took seven months; but in the end, as they moved relentlessly into position, the fate of Tyre was sealed.

Gaza, which did not present the same natural obstacles to be overcome fell in eight weeks. The occupation of the rest of Canaan followed smoothly. With the fall of Gaza the way was now open to Egypt, and here no defence was put up since, to the Egyptians, the conqueror appeared as a liberator from the Persian yoke. When in Egypt Alexander sacrificed piously to the gods of Memphis.

In Canaan all fell to him and all accepted his kingship, save the city of Jerusalem. In his march south he had not considered the place as lying in the line of his operations. The attitude of Jerusalem has been variously recorded, but it is generally accepted as deriving from allegiance to Persia, for the fidelity of the Jews to their oaths even when contracted with heathen princes was well recognized, and in the case of Persia they had reason to have strong feelings of indebtedness. They also supported Tyre in her resistance and Jeruslaem refused to accept Alexander's suzerainty there, even after the rest of Canaan had done so.

The Samarian version of Alexander's visit to the Holy City is that it was they who took him there, to see for himself the defiance of the Jewish priesthood. While he overlooked the place from a hill to the north known today as Mount Scopus, a procession all in white came out from the gate. Enquiring what this was, the Samaritans told him these were the rebels who denied his authority. To their astonishment and amazement of all who stood around Alexander descended from his chariot and bowed before the High Priest, saying that it was not to the priest he bowed but to the god whom he represented, further that he had had a vision of this before he departed from his homeland

This paying homage to the gods of the people he had conquered was part of a considered plan and was consistent with his conduct at Memphis. The meeting of Greek and Jew is of great significance, for, from this moment, Alexander became a symbol of union, and the commencement of a fraternity between the two races dates from this incident.

For the purpose of government Alexander included Canaan in what he called Coele-Syria, which in fact extended from the Taurus through the Lebanon to Egypt. The whole area he placed under the control of the Macedonian general, Parmenio, a distinguished soldier and politician. He fought gallantly under Philip and first made his name by a great victory over the Illyrians in 336. He was also one of the Macedonian delegates to negotiate and conclude the peace between Macedon and Athens. He led the left wing of Alexander's army in the battles of Granicus and Issus, and it was he who stood by the king's side at the historic scene outside Jerusalem. He did not hold the province for long, neither did his successor, Andromachus, who was burned alive by the Samaritans. For the Jews this had important consequences as Alexander in punishment settled Macedonians in the city of Samaria and, at the same time, granted the Jews the Samaritan territory as a form of reward for their loyalty to him.

By his settlement of the Levant and Egypt Alexander had sealed the fate of the Persian fleet. He was now free to complete the task of liquidating the Persian army and Darius's empire; but first, he went to Tyre where he concluded the final arrangements for the security of Coele-Syria. Crossing the River Tigris some four miles from Nineveh he met Darius, who was waiting for him with an immense army mustered from what was left of his empire. Here Darius intended to make his supreme effort, but at the subsequent battle, fought at Arbela, he was again and, by the same tactics, defeated. He fled the battlefield a fugitive and this marked the final collapse of the first Persian empire.

Having achieved his object in Persia Alexander now marched on India; but his further exploits here are not part of this story. In the far off land of India in June 323, at the age of thirty-two and eleven years after he had crossed the Hellespont, the greatest of all conquerors died.

The lesson of his triumph in the military field and of Persia's fall is that bravery and soldierly virtues are not enough, neither do numbers of themselves count. Superior intellect will prevail when this is accompanied by adequate leadership. Tactical methods must change and be suited both to the ground and the tactics of one's opponent. The Persian experience of Plataea should have told them their weaknesses; but it did not.

One of the objects of Alexander's military conquests had been the spread of the Hellenic culture. How did he set about effecting this? He came into the Asiatic world inspired with the belief that he was the great reconciler of the world. Union and not conquest was his goal. This could be achieved by three methods; first, the spread of the Greek language as the common vehicle for communication; second, the dissemination of Greek philosophy and culture; and third, the building of cities on the Greek model (or the development of old cities) with all the associated civic forms of government and administration.

The classic example of the Greek city was, of course, Alexandria. This city became the capital of the East, having a far wider influence on cultural thought than Babylon ever had. It was the centre of the world of that day, and it was the point at which Greek philosophy and the teachings of the Old Testament met in lasting union. Cities on the Greek lines sprang up in the train of Alexander's armies in Canaan, across Syria and on to the East.

The effects on Greece of the repulse and of the final defeat of Persia were, of course, profound for they heralded what has aptly been called 'The Great Age of Greece.' Their conquests gave these hardy people a sense of mission; they also gave material benefits; and they united a hitherto very independent series of states. Although it was a Macedonian who led, it was a united people that stood behind him. Alexander created an empire in Asia, and so the horizon of Hellenic vision spread far and wide, southwards to Upper Egypt and eastwards beyond the Indus. The Asian empire grew to great proportions; but eventually it separated itself from Greece, either, as in the case of Egypt as a friendly ally, or, as with the Seleucids as a rival.

The lofty conception of Alexander did not take shape. How was it that the grand ideal of unity which he dreamed of withered so quickly and among the very people from which he came and whom he had so gloriously led?

The fault, and fault there was, lay with the generals. Generals are great men in war; but when war is over they may not always be the right men for government. They may be very capable administrators, and indeed their military training should and does fit them well for such office; but there is a vast difference between capable administration and government with the responsibilities this entails. Ptolemy, Alexander's most capable and favourite general, one of his personal bodyguard and a great captain in battle; Antigonus Cyclops, another successful commander in war; and Seleucus, yet another of his leading generals, were no exceptions to this rule. All were strong characters, all trusted comrades and all men of great experience.

Let us now see how they reacted on the death of their master. We shall trace their actions and see how selfish motives and personal ambition split what started off as, and should have continued to be, one of the greatest empires of all time. In spite of them, the civilization which the cult of Hellenism introduced took root; but the political hegemony was broken up and the political divisions they set up left a scar, the mark of which remained for centuries.

A career as meteoric as Alexander's, cut off when the leader was in the midstream of a vast campaign and far away from his native land, was bound to leave a vacuum. His son, born shortly after his father's death, could not exert any influence. As a compromise his uncle, Philip, was elected to be joint king with the child, and both were placed under the guardianship of Perdiccas.

However, they were never able to wield real power, for that had in fact been seized by the generals who, meeting in Babylon after the king's death, under the influence of Ptolemy made their own plans for the settlement of the empire. Whilst recognizing, in a half-hearted way, the joint kingship of the child Alexander and Philip, the generals in point of fact divided the empire among themselves into three great satrapies; Egypt going to Ptolemy; Phrygia, the province of Pamphylia and Lycia going to Antigonus Cyclops; and Babylon and the East to Saleucus. Only the mainland of Greece and Macedon seem to have been left exclusively to Alexander and Philip. Here was dismemberment with a vengeance. Departed was the strong guiding hand, gone was centralized control, and gone was any hope of a united policy. Here were all the makings for keen competition, for jealousies, and ultimately for warring factions.

This division of Alexander's empire was momentous for Canaan. History was about to repeat itself, for once more the land was to find itself the bridge between rival and often warring kingdoms. This state of affairs was aptly summarized by Daniel who, although referred to as a prophet, was rather an historian. He wrote—'The king of the south shall be strong . . . for the king of the north shall return.' Indeed the kingdoms of the Ptolemies and the Seleucids passed to and fro with their great armies, their court intrigues and their pomp, their elephants, their cavalry and all their finery. Judaea at first remained aloof, but her isolationism could not last for long as the priesthood and most of the population inevitably became affected by what was going on all around them. Where did her interests lie? Could she remain united or would the conflict once more split her asunder? Before we can answer these questions we must first examine the consequences of the divisions these generals had of their own volition created.

First, Ptolemy appointed himself Satrap of Egypt under the two nominal kings of Greece, a pretence that he abandoned when, in 311, the young Alexander was murdered in Macedon. Ptolemy and his successors continued an uninterrupted rule in Egypt until the year A.D. 30, a period of two hundred and eighty years. Ptolemy's first and principal objective was to entrench his position in the Nile Valley and this he successfully did. After that he set out to gain possession of Cyprus and Coele-Syria. He quickly established a protectorate over the former and then invaded Canaan.

In the meantime Antigonus Cyclops had seized Syria and secured himself firmly in the valleys of the Tigris and Euphrates. He took possession of Susa and then occupied the city of Babylon, as a result of which Saleucus was forced to flee to Egypt, where he sought, and gained, the protection of Ptolemy. Antigonus then attacked Egypt where, at the fateful battle of Gaza, Ptolemy and Saleucus defeated Antigonus's army, at the time commanded by his son, Demetrius. Ptolemy, probably wisely, then decided to withdraw to Egypt and leave Antigonus free to do as he liked in Asia Minor, Syria and Babylon. At a stiff battle fought at Ipsus, Seleucus defeated Antigonus who was killed. This cleared the way for Seleucus, who now set about establishing what was to become famous as the Seleucid kingdom. He never forgave Ptolemy for what he considered the latter's desertion of him, and this ill-will was the start and basis of war between the kingdom of the north and the kingdom of the south.

Where the beautiful Orontes River bends to wind its way through the coastal plains and eventually empty itself into the Mediterranean, Seleucus founded a city, to which he gave the name Antioch, after his father, Antiochus. It was a city which, strangely enough, was destined ultimately to owe much of its celebrity not to Hellenic but to Semitic associations; for it was to Antioch that Barnabas took Saul and it was there that the disciples for a whole year were assembled. However, in the times we are now dealing with, Antioch was a very different place. As a capital city it vied with Alexandria; but whereas the latter can with justice be said to have represented commerce, learning and all the noble elements of an ancient civilization, Antioch represented splendour, luxury and the vanities of the ancient Babylon. The early relations between the Jews and Alexandria were intellectually sympathetic, breeding a natural friendship with the Ptolemies; whereas the Seleucid capital at Antioch was antipathetic to the Jews whose relations with the northern kingdom were, not surprisingly, somewhat antagonistic.

To the people of Judaea the strength and the friendship of the southern kingdom was of material interest. A large portion of their displaced population had made their home in Egypt and a settlement had grown up on the east side of Alexandria close along the seashore, where the Jews had been permitted to retain privileges on the same level as those of the Macedonian settlers. Here the former became a tightly-knit community which later formed a third of the city's total population.

Desultory war between the Ptolemies and the Seleucids continued until, in 223, Antiochus the Great succeeded to the northern throne. In the second year of his reign he made a serious attempt to invade Canaan this time, however, to be bettered by Ptolemy III. Later, in 218, he made a more successful bid in which he captured Philoteria on the Sea of Galilee,

Scythopolis, Philadelphia and Gaza. In the following year Ptolemy regained some of the lost territories, some of the Jews supporting him and some Antiochus. This attitude of the Jews is of more than passing interest, for it showed a state of mind in which opportunism and not conviction had begun to influence their actions, which Polybius later wrote of as indicating that they were too ready to accommodate themselves to the situation of the moment and too prone to meaningless courtesies when it suited them.

On the death of Ptolemy Philopater, a weak man to whose ineffectual reign much of the success of Antiochus was due, the Seleucid king seized the opportunity to make a further bid for Canaan in which, this time, he was successful and was supported by sections of the Jews. Near Paneas, at the source of the Jordan, he inflicted a heavy defeat on the Egyptian army. Strong in his possessions Antiochus was now able to make a secret treaty with Philip of Macedon by which it was agreed that he should have suzerainty over Asia Minor, Syria and Canaan as well as over the territories up to and including the Euphrates. Only Egypt was left to the Ptolemies. Truly the kings of the north had returned. Seleucid power was now at its height.

The truce with Egypt Antiochus was constrained to make was at the instigation of Rome. This is, therefore, the right moment to bring this great country into the picture.

By now Rome had become mistress of a large part of Eastern Europe, and, by her victory over Hannibal at the battle of Zama, she had sealed the fate of Western Europe. Carthage was broken and its power passed to the Romans who were now directing their attentions towards Asia. For many years Rome had enjoyed a sort of alliance with the Ptolemies which was built up largely on trade and commerce. Egypt had supplied Rome with grain during the Punic wars and this act had cemented friendship between the two. It was, therefore, only natural that any aggressive action against Egypt would be likely to arouse resentment in Rome. In the case of Antiochus the matter was dealt with by diplomatic methods.

For many years the Illyrian pirates had worried both Roman and Greek shipping and so, when the Romans thoroughly chastized the ravaging seamen, they were consolidating their already friendly relations with the Greeks whose learning, philosophy and wisdom the Romans long had admired. Antiochus's ambitions foolishly drove him into attacking Greece and so he found himself at war with Rome. At Thermopylae, he was defeated and, in a treaty signed at Apasnea, was forced to give up all his territories north of the Taurus, only retaining Canaan.

From now, Rome was the dominant power in the Near East.

15 The first resistance movement

This is the story of a resistance movement which, commencing with the oppressions of Antigonus Epiphanes, culminated with the fall and sack of Jerusalem. There were many factors at play the principal ones were the brutality of Antiochus, the schism among the Jews, and the character of the Herods and of their Roman masters.

Antiochus was a man of complex character; evil and good, he was known by the two names Epiphanes, the 'manifest' (i.e. god) and Epimanes, the madman. He combined the ideals of a lofty thought with petty and vicious actions. He considered himself one of the gods of Greece and was an egoist who would stand no opposition to his fixed objectives. The most important of these was to bring all his realm into complete submission to himself and to the gods of Greece.

Many Jews now belonged to the Hellenistic party. The fever for Greek fashion showed itself in the adoption of Macedonian names; Solomon became Alexander, Onias and Mattathias respectively Menelaus and Antigonus. These things, though not necessarily of great significance in themselves, were none the less an indication of the influence Hellenistic cult was beginning to have on this hitherto exclusive and conservative race.

More disturbing, however, was the increase in the desire to adopt Greek manners. The modesty of many of the elderly Jews was shocked by the establishment under the very citadel of David of the Greek Palaestra, where the more active of the youths leaped completely naked in public sports, wrestling and running with only the broad-brimmed hat, the headgear of the god Hermes, the guardian of gymnastic festivals. Even some of the priests became affected leaving their devotions to witness the throwing of the quoit, the signal for commencement of the games.

One Jew who epitomized all that was worst in what was taking place was Jason. He it was who offered Antiochus a bribe to allow him to attempt the conversion of Jerusalem into a Greek city, and it was under him that the Greek gymnasium was set up outside the temple and the Greek guilds encouraged among the younger generation.

The Jews were at the cross-roads. Were the teachings of the prophets to be discarded in favour of the pagan rites of Athens? Were the heathen trappings of Antioch to replace the dignity of Alexandria, where the fusion of the best of Greek learning and ancient Hebrew philosophy had begun so auspiciously? The mass of the people were beginning to wonder how far down the deadly slope of compromise they were to be led. Was there, in fact, any room for compromise?

In the midst of all this conflict the true character of Antiochus now displayed itself. The start of his ruthless activities against the Jews stemmed from a set-back he experienced in Egypt. Animated by his ego, and misjudging Roman reaction, he made plans for the invasion of the Nile Delta. Some indication of the power of Rome and the influence she had can be gleaned from the fact that it took merely the intervention of the Roman ambassador to turn the would-be conqueror in his tracks. Reluctant though he was, Antiochus bowed his head to authority and withdrew his army; but what hurt him most was that he was compelled to give up his important garrison at Pelusium. The consequence of the loss of this outpost was that, in compensation, he felt impelled to strengthen his position in southern Canaan, and to this end decided to seize Jerusalem, which he did, placing a garrison in a new fortress on Mount Zion.

He now, in a most callous manner, proceeded to outrage the Jewish susceptibilities. The worship of Yahweh was forbidden and in the Holy Place the worship of Zeus Olympius was ordered. At every town and village in the land altars were erected to the pagan gods at which the wretched inhabitants were compelled to sacrifice. The cherished customs of repose on the sabbath and of circumcision were forbidden. The great carved gates of the temple were burned. As though this were not enough, the licentious rites of Antioch were performed in the courts of the temple, and these were permitted to become overgrown with grass and weed. These profanities were consumated by placing a herd of swine in the precincts and in the Holy of Holies. Daily offerings ceased and the Perpetual Light was extinguished. This surely was the abomination of desolation.

Horrible as it may seem, and difficult as it may be to understand, many Jews bowed before and even assisted in this oppression. Mariam, the daughter of a priestly order, who had married an officer in the Syrian army, kicked the altar with her shoes asking how much longer was it to consume the wealth of the Jews. Nevertheless, in spite of all, there were those who were prepared to defy and to refuse to submit.

These people hid in caves in the Hills of Judaea like their forbears in the days of the Philistines, and from these they were smoked out or burned to death. Mothers who refused to submit were hanged with their babies at their breasts, and Eleazar, a venerable scribe of over ninety years, was put on the rack and scourged to death.

Such a period of persecution was bound to raise a resistance, and the first sparks of this came in a small village called Modin in the hills of the Shephelah, that debatable land that had for centuries been a field of battle.

The head of a priestly family, one Mattathias, had left Jerusalem as a result of the paganism practised there and moved to his house at Modin. Amidst its beautiful surroundings from its roof glimpses of the blue sea could be had, while on the Judaean hills the setting sun threw gentle lights and long shadows. Such was Mattathias's home. But, as was happening throughout the whole country, an altar had been erected near his house at which the people were ordered to sacrifice. The old man refused to have anything to do with the pagan rites and, as he stood and saw one of his own countrymen complying with the hatred order, his anger was intense. In a rage he set about the man and the royal officer who was supervising the sacrifice. He was then forced to flee into the hills for safety, and from here he raised a war cry. He, his sons and his little band, were forced to live like hunted animals; but they planned, and from these hills developed their great movement of resistance.

Wherever they found a pagan altar they raided and destroyed it, and if they heard of an uncircumcised child they would circumcise it. People began to flock to them until eventually they became strong enough to fight Antiochus's generals, whom they drove out of Judaea. His watchword was to fight, and the people made Mattathias their prince. From these beginnings and in this way was the great Asmonean dynasty founded. Born in strife, though it reached great heights, it eventually died in tragedy as this story will unfold.

Mattathias lived only for a short time after these successes, the hardships he had endured and his age took their unevitable toll. He died, but not until he had lit a torch that he was to hand on to his sons. These were to succeed him in turn and the family to rule for one hundred and thirty years.

The Asmoneans were men of valour who, for the most part, were inspired by the finest ideals; they were often brilliant and all, perhaps with one exception, were ambitious. They had strong characters, were picturesque, romantic and of grand physique. They enjoyed good health and the joy of life shone in their eyes. Their women were as great as their men, possessing beauty, courage and steadfastness that was epitomized in the sad life of Mariamne, destined to be the last of the true Asmoneans.

16 The Maccabaean wars

Mattathias had five sons, all of whom were robust and all worthy members of a great family. At his behest the old man was followed as leader by the third son, Judas Maccab or Judas the Hammer. Judas was succeeded by his younger brother, Jonathan, who in turn was followed by their elder brother, Simon. Mattathias had shown the way, and Judas, Jonathan and Simon, each in his turn helped to establish a kingdom which achieved international status, a kingdom destined to be the ally of the greatest power in the Western world, Rome.

Mattathias died in the year 167 and Simon thirty years after. In this span of time the Jews from being a small, unimportant and hounded community living insecurely around Jerusalem and in the hills of Judaea, had become a nation comparable both in size and in importance with that of David. After Simon the dynasty carried on successively under the kingship of John Hyrcanus, Aristobulus and Alexander Jannaeus, but when, in 69, Hyrcanus II came to rule a decline set in. This decline was inevitable, for circumstances far beyond his control were at work. The direct line was extinguished with the execution of Mariamne and the house finished with the murder of her two sons.

When Judas Maccab followed his father the people had as a leader a truly lovable and remarkable character. Before everything else he was cheerful, known to his friends as the happy warrior. Few have struck the popular imagination as did this Judas. In the military sphere of all chiefs he surely with the most scanty means accomplished the greatest ends. He raised his people from the brink of extinction to a higher level of freedom than any could remember. His cheerful smile ran like a tonic through the ranks of those he led, and his voice, like that of a lusty lion, gave both confidence and cheer. Long did his people recall his grand appearance when, clad in his armour, like a giant he would tighten his belt and wave his great sword, exalting the hearts of his faithful followers. They longed to hear his voice; they exulted over his victories; and they adored him for his chivalry. Never was knight in armour more esteemed or more loved.

Those who rallied to him were in an unenviable position. They had to fight a war on two fronts; against those of their own blood who preferred Hellenism to orthodoxy, and against the powerful king of the north, Antiochus Epiphanes, besides whose strength they were but a puny band. On the face of it they could not hope by resistance to achieve much more than small tactical successes, to carry out minor raids and sabotage, and to achieve even these limited objections mainly by surprise. But the desperation that had given birth to the movement called for more than this. To overcome the tyranny of Antiochus and to stamp out the Hellenistic cult demanded nothing short of all-out war. Thus a resistance movement developed, as it had to, into a great campaign.

Judas's early battles took place in and around the hills near his home. Here, in the first two years, he gained three decisive victories, and these, to a frustrated people, were a tonic indeed.

His first success was against Apollonius, a general whose forces he surprised near Samaria, only twenty miles to the north of his home. It was here that he himself captured the sword of Apollonius which he kept, as David had Goliath's, and carried into battle to the end of his life.

His second victory was near Beth Horon, some six miles to

the east of Modin, but of the details of this engagement little is known.

The third, however, had the most far-reaching effects. The Syrian army, then under the command of the famous general, Nicanor, was encamped at Emmaus and present were Lysias, the governor of the province, and Antiochus, the king's son. The king himself at this time was absent in Persia. Judas had moved his men up to the high ground at Mizpah from where they could see Jerusalem. He addressed his soldiers telling them of his intentions. For success surprise must be his principal weapon. The Syrians knew that at Mizpah he was in a strong position; what, therefore, was less likely than that he should leave this? Next, he proposed to divide his force into four columns, one under himself, one under Simon and the other two under Jonathan and John respectively. The attack was to be carried out under cover of darkness, the four columns giving the impression of greater numbers than he had.

So, moving swiftly and silently, he and his men descended from the hills and advanced on the unsuspecting Syrians. When they woke to hear the blast of the Maccabee's trumpets and to be assaulted simultaneously from four sides the Syrians were thrown into confusion. Judah's men plunged into their camp which they set on fire. As dawn broke pillars of smoke could be seen rising from the now deserted encampment where, only a few hours before, a great army had been sleeping in presumed safety.

Colesthenes, the man who had set fire to the wooden pillars of the temple, they captured and, forcing him into a wooden hut, burned him alive. The battle had started on a Friday and the sabbath had now set in; Judas called off the pursuit. Perhaps he was influenced more by military caution than by religious custom.

These three successes raised the morale of those in the resistance movement; but of greater importance even than this was their effect on the people as a whole. To them it was the first ray of hope; hope that the oppression from which they so sorely suffered might come to an end; hope that the freedom of worship now denied them might be restored; and hope that Yahweh would once again save them and re-raise them to a state of nationhood.

Much more had to be done before these hopes could be fulfilled. Jerusalem was barred to them and the temple still desecrated. The hated garrison was on Mount Zion, and the road to the city was patrolled from the strong Syrian garrison at Beth Sur, thirteen miles distant from Jerusalem. Beth Sur was a natural fortress at the head of the road from the coastal plain which, following the Vale of Elah (a name derived from the ilex trees with which it abounded), bends south at the valley of the Sur rising steeply to the fortress. Beth Sur was commanded by Lysias himself.

Judas, unabashed by the strength of the position, but knowing every detail of the ground, advanced up the valley of the Sur and attacked the garrison. Once more he registered a success and the way to Jerusalem now lay open, only the small garrison at Mount Zion remaining; but this they were able to contain, for it was neither strong enough to eject them nor big enough to prevent the overjoyed soldiers from entering the Holy Place.

What a sight met their eyes. Everywhere was desolation and havoc. Torn down were the old chambers of the priests; the gates of the temple were but a pile of ashes; the altar was disfigured; and the whole area was overgrown with weed. Though their first reaction was to blow the loud horns and to celebrate the relief, more stern work had first to be done; so, keeping the small garrison at bay, they set about cleansing the filthy place. They washed everything that had been defiled by the swine; they removed the pagan altar and pagan statues; they even pulled down the great platform of the old altar, lest its stones should have been polluted. They then furnished the temple anew. Three years after the profanation, and on its anniversary, the temple was re-dedicated. The smoke once more ascended from the altar and, though they had to be content with iron stands in the place of the old golden candlesticks, the candles once more burned in the Holy Place.

The relief of Jerusalem by no means meant that the struggle was finished. Loyal Hebrews in Idumaea, that stretch of country to the south of Hebron, as well as those of their race in Gilead and in Galilee, had to be rescued from the Syrians and the pro-Hellenistic members of their own stock. Judas had now occupied the fortress at Beth Sur which he made the base for his operations in Idumaea and so, from the heights of Akrabbin, he swept down on the Children of the Bean, as the Arab tribes in that area were called. Into their villages and into their forts he went and all he destroyed. In the north, in engagement after engagement, he beat the Ammonites led by Timothius, eventually returning to Jerusalem in triumph. Timothius, however, was able to rally his forces and before long once again was harrying the non-Hellenistic Jews in Galilee and across the Jordan.

On hearing of the worsening plight of those in Galilee, Judas sent his brother, Simon, to their rescue. Simon's campaign was successful and he drove the Syrians as far as Ptolemais, the Acre of modern times. With another brother, Jonathan the Cunning, Judas marched to the rescue of those east of the Jordan. Here he arrived just in time, for Timotheus had completed his plans, which he was now about to put into effect, of besieging simultaneously a number of Hebrew strongholds into which the terrified people had fled. Even the scaling ladders were in position and battering rams ready when, in the dawn, the clarion trumpet blast of the Maccabees was heard. The results were electric; the sieges were raised and the enemy fled; such by now was the reputation of 'The Hammer of the Gentiles.' This time Judas relentlessly pursued the Syrians across the heights of Gilead and across the Jordan into Galilee. While they were still disorganized he attacked and defeated them on the famous battle-field near the Horns of Hattin. On his return he crossed the Jordan once again and, after one more sally to the south, he completed this splendid *tour de force* by capturing the important city of Hebron, which up till then the Syrians had held.

However difficult the tasks that lay ahead, the Maccabees had by now turned the corner and ultimate success, which before had seemed impossibly difficult to achieve, was within their grasp. An event now played into their hands, the king Antiochus Epiphanes died. This was in the year 164. Few mourned his passing. At his death civil war broke out in his kingdom and his son, Antiochus, having to fight for his life was ultimately killed by his uncle, Demetrius, who then seized the throne. This rift in the enemy camp was a blessing for the Maccabees, but its potential advantage was sadly offset by lack of co-operation in the Hebrew ranks. Alcimus (Jakim), the High Priest, maintained his position by grace of Antioch and, incredible as this may seem, was in active opposition to Judas.

As though this were not enough Judas now suffered his first military defeat when the fortress of Beth Sur fell to the enemy. A large Syro-Greek army, which included many elephants introduced into the army by Alexander the Great, advanced on the stronghold. Toiling up the Vale of Elah these magnificent brutes must have been an inspiring sight. Each had a wooden tower erected on its back and their gaudily dressed Indian mahouts, sitting between their ears, gave an added stamp of oriental pomp to the impression of strength that these brutes inspired. With each marched a strong phalanx of heavily armed infantry behind which followed five hundred cavalry. The soldiers were all equipped with shields and helmets of brass. Never had the Vale witnessed such a magnificent spectacle as the sun shone on shields and spears and the whole area glistened with their reflected light.

The battle for Beth Sur was fierce, but the conclusion was inevitable. Magnificent in attack when they could surprise their foe, the Maccabees were in no class to meet in defence the assault of such a powerful army. Their defeat was relieved by the epic of Judas's brother, Eleazar, who paid the price of his life for his gallant act. Singling out an elephant on which he thought the prince was riding, he fought his way through the ranks and, reaching the beast, with one thrust of his sword pierced its belly, bringing the mighty animal down on himself.

Nicanor was now chosen to conduct the next phase of the operations against the Maccabees and part of this plan was to reoccupy the city of Jerusalem. Nicanor had always had a great regard for the Maccabaean leader and so he sought an opportunity to talk to him. Judas was suspicious but in the end agreed to meet him. When the two men came face to face each recognized in the other qualities that drew them together. It was a meeting of two great men and, as they sat together, Nicanor was completely fascinated by Judas. He asked him why he did not give up leading his present life and settle down, marry and have some children of his own. Strangely, Judas seemed inclined to listen to this advice, for he did marry and for a time settle down.

The real tragedy of these times was now revealed in all its petty rottenness. The High Priest Alcimus, seeing in this apparent friendship a danger to his own aspirations, denounced Nicanor to the king at Antioch; he even went further than this and procured an order for Judas to be sent a prisoner to the capital, making out that Nicanor had instigated this. This split the friendship. Seeing what he thought was the writing on the wall, Judas was from now suspicious of Nicanor. After a small skirmish between him and the royal troops in the Plain of Sharon, the friendship, which had not lasted long but which seemed to have boded so much good, broke up. It was never formed again.

Not long after Judas and Nicanor met in serious battle. This time it was at Beth Horon, the scene of the previous engagement and near Modin. Nicanor was advancing on Jerusalem up the valley that passed the Asmonean's home, and so once again Judas was in country dearly loved by him and his devoted followers. In the battle he scored one of his greatest successes, for Nicanor was slain and the Syrian army completely routed. The battle was long, the fighting severe and the result in the balance, but the loss of their general tipped the balance and with it the Syrian resistance collapsed. Among the gory trophies that the victors carried to Jerusalem was Nicanor's right hand, the one that he had stretched out when he said he would destroy the Holy City. This was Judas's last military success.

One mark of his keen perception had been his appreciation of the ever increasing importance of Rome and so, in 162, he sent emissaries to the Senate. This is some indication of the width of his vision and of the position he had carved out for himself and his people. His emissaries were received with all the courtesies and dignities accorded by one sovereign power to another. The outcome was an alliance which was ratified and recorded on two tablets of brass, one of which was deposited in the Tabularium beneath the Capitol and the other sent to Jerusalem. However, before it arrived at the Holy City its bold instigator was slain in battle; nevertheless, its fruits remained for from this moment Roman interest in Canaan was aroused. Though control followed later the interest, though friendly, was at first hesitant; the more oppressive weight of Rome and Roman rule was as yet a hundred years away. After the defeat of Nicanor and with these negotiations completed Judas had opened a wider vista for his country than any had dreamed possible. With his new and powerful ally he had every reason for quiet confidence. But fate was to play against him.

The Syrians sent a new army under the command of Bacchides to avenge the defeat of Nicanor. This army advanced on Jerusalem by the Jordan route. Judas, as usual, called on the people to rally, setting out himself to intercept the foe. But, thanks to the incredibly base machinations of Alcimus and of members of a stiff-necked sect later to be called the Pharisees, he was not supported. The famous trumpet sounded for the last time. His followers fought a losing battle that raged from morning until night, but with odds heavily against them, the end was inevitable. Judas was killed, and his dead body removed to the ancestral sepulchre at Modin.

With the passing of Judas a phase had now ended. Gone was a hero, a leader and an inspired man. Though his brothers were there to carry on the torch, for a time after his death his successor, Jonathan the Cunning, was forced to take refuge in the hills. Soon, however, two events were to play into his hands. The first was the sudden death of the High Priest, Alcimus; the second was occasioned by rivalries for the throne at Antioch.

Opposing Demetrius was a usurper, Alexander Belas, to whom Jonathan gave his support. When Alexander seized the throne, in return for this support, he made Jonathan High Priest in the place of Alcimus. On conferring this office on Jonathan he referred to him as the king's friend, and presented him with the golden crown and purple robe, the marks of regal state.

In the military field Jonathan had had successes against Demetrius's general, Bacchides. When in 158 the latter returned once more to Judaea, Jonathan with his brother Simon, defeated the Syrian at the siege of Bathbesi. The Syrian's army now challenged his rights in the Plain of Philistia and here, in a series of engagements, Jonathan's archers beat the enemy cavalry with heavy losses. Askalon, Joppa, Lydda, and Ramathaim all fell to him.

Sixteen years after succeeding Judas, and nine years after becoming High Priest and king, he met his death at the hand of a Syrian, Typhon, in an obscure village east of the Jordan. When one considers the apparent hopelessness of his position on succeeding his brother it is remarkable what this man achieved. If the cards of fortune were favourable he certainly knew how to play them. When he died Jonathan had secured religious freedom; Jerusalem also was freed; Syrian military power had been kept in check; the position of king and High Priest had been established; and his country was recognized as a viable state.

He was succeeded by his elder brother, Simon, of whom old Mattathias said he was the father of them all. Simon rose to great occasions; and, though well advanced in years, he had many fine military achievements. The Syrians still held the city of Gezer, the fortress at Beth Sur and the post on Mount Zion. Simon retook Gezer and there established a Jewish colony under his son, John Hyrcanus; he then took and re-occupied Beth Sur; and finally he expelled the Syrians from the citadel overlooking the Sanctuary which had for so long wounded Hebrew pride.

Nevertheless, his fame did not rest solely on his military actions. Hebrew contracts now bore the date and heading, '. . . the year of Simon, the Great High Priest and General and Leader of the Jews.' In the fourth year of his reign he was able to strike his own coinage, while to Rome he sent his ambassador, a matter that did not go unnoticed at Antioch. In spite of all that he did tragedy overtook him, for in 135, seventeen years after his succeeding his brother, he and his two younger sons were entrapped by his son-in-law in the fortress of Dok, near Jericho, where they were brutally murdered. On hearing of this plot, the eldest son, John Hyrcanus, came post haste from Gezer to Jerusalem, where he gained possession of the city before the plotters could reach it, and when he was immediately recognized as Simon's successor.

John Hyrcanus had a long and prosperous reign lasting some twenty-six years. Though initially he had still to admit a degree of Syrian control, this he was later able to renounce. When Antiochus Sidetes, now on the throne at Antioch, was killed in his ill-fated expedition against the Parthians, John Hyrcanus felt Syria could be defied. He overran Samaria and then invaded Edom, whose people he forced to accept circumcision, on the basis of recognition of their original Hebrew status; a step that was later to have repercussions which he could never at the time have foreseen.

East of the Jordan he secured Mediba and in the north he captured Scythopolis. He retook Jezreel and then, turning south, he attacked Samaria, razing the city to the ground and with it the hated temple of Gerizim.

He was succeeded by his son Aristobulus, who after a short reign died, to be followed by his brother, Alexander Jannaeus. The new king was able to continue the successes of his predecessors. With the exception of the city of Ptolemais, which remained Greek, he annexed all the sea coast as far south as Gaza, and all the settlements across Jordan, whether Greek or Arab, came under his control.

His difficulties were, however, on the home front, and particularly with the orthodox Jews, who resented his incursions into the provinces of the gentiles. He unfortunately suffered a reverse at the hands of Obodas, the king of Arabia, and this the hostile elements in Jerusalem used to instigate a revolt against him. This was led by the Pharisees, who revived a sordid scandal concerning his grandmother. Later, at the Feast of Tabernacles, the Pharisees whipped up the worshippers in the temple to such an extent that they pelted him as High Priest with fruit from the branches of the citrus trees they carried on that day.

With the rage of a lion Alexander Jannaeus sought his revenge, no less than six thousand people paying for the insult with their lives. Things got worse and when the Pharisees, with the viciousness of fanatics, sided with the Syrian king against him he stormed the fortress in which they took refuge, ordering the execution by crucifixion of eight hundred of their leaders.

On his death he was succeeded by his wife. Her reign, which lasted for ten years, was remarkable since it was the first time in the history of these people that a woman reigned. She could, of course, not be High Priest to which office she appointed her son, Hyrcanus. This step had far-reaching results, for by custom the High Priest would on her death be king, and thus did not coincide with the views of the other son, Aristobulus, who laid claim to the throne himself. This thus became the cause of strife which on the queen's death resulted in civil war. The consequences of this were far-reaching and involved the intervention of Rome, an intervention which the sons themselves called for when they appealed to Pompey to judge their respective claims.

With the queen's passing, though the family continued for some time, the great age of the Maccabees came to an end.

From a point of almost extermination a small religious community in remote Judaea rose to be a power respected throughout the Near East. A small resistance movement, spiritually inspired and with a people behind it, had achieved the apparently impossible. This astounding family had regained for the Jews something if not all of the greatness of the Kingdom of David of old.

17 Rome comes to Canaan

Before considering the local effects of the rivalry between the two princes it will be well to remark on the position Rome now held in Asia. When Antiochus the Great overstepped the mark in Greece Rome assumed a protectorate role over the Greek possessions in Asia Minor. She also established friendly relations with the Greek cities in Canaan with some of which she concluded friendly independent alliances. Secure now in the absence of any formidable threat to her position she lapsed into inactivity with near disastrous results.

First, her trade was harassed by the pirates in the eastern Mediterranean, who achieved almost complete command of the sea. Next, the growing power of Mithradates of Pontus threatened her position in Asia.

It was to settle the issues of the pirates and the threat from Mithradates that Pompey in the year 63 was sent from Rome. Against the former he scored quick successes while on land he was victorious against Mithridates whom he forced to flee the country. It was at this stage and at the height of his military career that Pompey enters this story.

When, through the initiative of Judus, the Maccabees first came in contact with Rome the impressions they created were excellent. These impressions were strengthened during the reign of Simon. The main picture that the Romans had was of a kingdom with a sincere and serious outlook on religion, coupled with a peculiarly sacred view of the office of kingship and government. It was left to the sagacious eye of Tacitus later to see beneath the surface the darker shadows of strife, jealousies and rapaciousness that were latent in the Jews at that time. Pompey probably had a high opinion of these people who for the first time he was about to meet.

Aristobulus seized the throne from his elder brother immediately his mother died, and a state amounting to civil war set in. Knowing that Pompey was about to enter Damascus, the two brothers decided to put their case for arbitration to the victorious Roman general.

Gnaeus Pompeius Magnus, Triumvir, was born on 30th of September 106, so that after his defeat of the Parthians and Mithridates and at the time of this story he was in his early forties. There was in the outward appearance of this man something compelling. His august expression conveyed an impression of almost venerable dignity, which was nevertheless blended with the bloom of a man in his physical prime. He had an engaging manner that charmed all whom he met. His brow was smooth and he had a kind but penetrating eye. His victories in Africa, in Spain and against the pirates in the Mediterranean, coupled with his achievement in establishing Roman supremacy in Asia had made him a hero. He had also earned a reputation for moderation and this made him a fitting arbitrater for the contending princes. It was said of him that though he might not know how to restrain those under him, he gave such a gracious reception to those who came to him that they went away satisfied. Such was the man the two had put their faith in.

But what of the two princes? The one, Aristobulus, a true Asmonean in character was gallant, having a high spirit that called for admiration even among his critics. He loved to surround himself with pomp and had in his entourage young nobles gay in their apparel, their mantles and their clustering locks. On the other hand, his elder brother, Hyrcanus, was insignificant, of weak character and easily influenced.

To the proud but simple Roman soldier the oriental pomp and extravagance of Aristobulus were nauseating and it was, therefore, with something of an initial sympathy that he turned to Hyrcanus. Disliking the one, and feeling that the other would in all probability be the more malleable, he decided to support Hyrcanus.

When, some fifty years earlier, John Hyrcanus had subdued the hardy Edomites little did he foresee that by incorporating these people into the Jewish faith and making Herod (Antipas) the first governor of Idumaea he was giving the kiss of death to his own house. It was this Herod's son, another Antipas, who pleaded Hyrcanus's cause now with Pompey. This same man, initially through the favour of Pompey and later of Caesar, became the first Roman Procurator of Judaea. Antipas, in pressing Hyrcanus's case, did so because he craftily perceived that his own ends would be better served if the weaker of the two was to be selected by Pompey.

It was most unlikely that the hot-headed Aristobulus would take kindly to Pompey's decision. He withdrew to his stronghold at Alexandrium, a fortress which commanded the road into Canaan. Here he planned to resist or at least force a parley with the Roman; but Pompey, a soldier and man of action, quickly followed him up and Aristobulus was forced to quit Alexandrium and flee to Jerusalem. Here he was virtually a prisoner. However, completely misjudging his man, he made the fatal error of thinking that once again he could defy Pompey. The Roman now moved on to the capital, not by the well-worn route through Bethel but by the Valley of the Jordan. He camped at Jericho and, while resting in the shade of the groves there, he received the unexpected and good news that his old enemy, Mithridates, had died in the Caucasus. His rear was now quite safe and this gave him freedom to proceed with his plans in Canaan. He marched on Jerusalem.

Approaching the city from this direction the sight of this naturally beautiful place had a deep effect on him; an inspiring sight, it was not lost on such an impressionable character.

Aristobulus, still hoping that he could persuade Pompey to change his mind, came out to meet him. This time, however, he received the treatment he had asked for, he was seized and bound a prisoner in chains. Then commenced another siege of the city, a siege that lasted three months and only terminated after upwards of twelve thousand people had lost their lives.

Now occurred an incident which to the Jews constituted an outrage; one, moreover, that neither Nebuchadrezzar nor Alexander the Great had seen fit to perpetrate. Pompey, drawn by some irresistible force and a desire to see with his own eyes that which no other had seen, entered the Holy of Holies. He walked into that part of the temple where none but the priests might enter. He touched nothing, he only looked in astonishment and reverence. He had been deeply moved and on the following day gave instructions that the contamination should be purified. But, fine though his character was and sincere though his feelings might have been, the harm was done. Later when he and Caesar quarrelled the Jews sided with his rival, in reality their enemy, Caesar. They could never find it in their hearts to forgive Pompey.

One frightening aspect of this fall of Jerusalem was that once again were the bitter conflicts between the sects of Jewry to be evidenced. The Sadducees, the custodians of the Law, were fixed in their determination to adhere to the written word and, because the assault on the temple took place on the sabbath, not a hand would they permit to be raised in its defence.

For the Romans the day of the capture of Jersualem was of such significance that the names of the officers who stormed the breach were recorded and remembered. Cornelius Faustus, son of Sulla, led the van and he was followed by the centurions Fabius and Furius.

After this Pompey divided the country into districts and the central government was abolished, to be replaced by five separate councils that sat with equal power at Jerusalem, Gadara, Amathus, Jericho and Sepphoris. It was with fitting sarcasm that Josephus wrote that the country passed from a monarchy to an aristocracy. As a distinct community the Jews were virtually confined to Judaea.

These sad events took place only twelve months after Pompey's meeting with the two princes at Damascus. Could they then have realized the possibilities they were opening up? This tragic and unnecessary quarrel resulting in Pompey's invited intervention, plus the rival factions in the Hebrew hegemony, spelt the ultimate dismemberment of a state which the Maccabees had with bloodshed and courage wisely built up. A state, moreover, that for one hundred years was held in high esteem far and wide, not only in the confines of Coele-Syria but in the great world beyond.

18 Herod the Great

The last of the great characters to take the stage in this historic scene prepares the way for the final drama. Power moved to Rome and the intransigent stand by both sides led ultimately to war; Herod, while he lived, bridged this gap. Nevertheless, his life was tragic and at times villainous, yet it would be wrong for history to deal too harshly with him.

How did he come to occupy such a vital position? Was he a great man or was he a villain? Did he deserve the epithet of 'great' which history has bestowed upon him?

When in 129 John Hyrcanus subdued the race of Esau and incorporated the Edomite tribes into the Hebrew nation he set in train a set of circumstances that eventually resulted in one of this race becoming King of the Jews. Herod the Great was born in 72 and was the son of Antipas who, as the second governor of the Edomite state, had with an eye on his own future supported the cause of Hyrcanus with Pompey. Flirting first with Pompey and subsequently with Caesar he had, as a Jew, worked his way into the high office of Roman procurator for Judaea. He was careful to groom his son for this position when his turn should come to succeed him, placing Herod, while still a youth, in charge of the district of Galilee which, deriving its name from the hilly nature of that border country, was the refuge of high spirited brigands.

The young Herod possessed a splendid appearance with his

fine black hair which he always kept most carefully groomed. There was a violent streak in his character that showed itself in his treatment of the bandits of Galilee and again, later in his life, when judgement gave way to fanatical cruelty. There was, nevertheless, in him a greatness of soul that at times raised him above petty jealousies and selfish ends. His family affections were deep, if not always lasting.

He was a man of high intellectual qualities, inquisitive and passionately interested in history and philosophy, who entered into the glories and pleasures of Greek and Roman art. He took a delight in beneficence, not only in Canaan but in all the cities of Greece and Syria. He repaired the temple of Apollo at Rhodes, showing thereby a toleration beyond his time that kindled the admiration of people even of his own race. In the cities of Syria and in Asia Minor he founded places for athletic exercise and in Canaan, near the source of the River Jordan at Dan, he built a marble temple which he dedicated to his patron and called it Caesarea-Philippi. On the spoiled site of Samaria, the place of his marriage to Mariamne, he built a noble city which he called Sebaste. On the coast he constructed a port for Sebaste and abutting on to it he built a city with an array of public and private edifices of shining marble. This city he called Caesarea. But the greatest of his works was the restored temple in Jerusalem, the life of which was to be so sadly short.

Herod set the stage on which men like Josephus, who ultimately were torn between their civilization and that of their Roman masters, were to play their part. He was a man of stature, whose life, when he was young, was full of promise. His subsequent actions, and indeed his whole character, owed much to his antecedents and the stock from which he came.

He sprang, of course, from Edomite origins, and the Edomites had retained the characteristics of their apocryphal father, Esau. In their wild nomadic life they were independent and proud; yet they possessed and nursed an inward grievance that bred the deepest of animosities. While, through force of arms, they had been compelled to bow to Israelite supremacy and more recently to bend the knee to John Hyrcanus, and while they were content to unite themselves with the descendants of Abraham by circumcision, they were impelled by ambition to rid themselves once and for all of their brothers' yoke. This was Herod's heritage.

Men who had the ambition of Antipas and Herod, skilled in war and adroit in politics, aimed, it is scarcely surprising to note, at power; and, when they achieved it, they used their position with a ruthlessness as skilfully applied as it was terrible in its consequences.

When Herod was in Galilee his arbitrary way of dealing with the local brigands had brought him into open conflict with the elders in Jerusalem. One of the robber leaders, Hezekiah, who was in the eyes of the local people a hero, fell into Herod's hands and was summarily executed. This was an infringement of the prerogative of the Sanhedrin, who promptly cited Herod in the name of Hyrcanus to appear before them. He came before the court, not as a suppliant clothed in black with hair combed down, but as a splendid youth, surrounded by a bodyguard of his own soldiers. The governor of Antioch intervened and ordered his acquittal. Such was Herod and such the authority of Rome.

However, when on his father's death he succeeded to the procuratorship all did not go well with him. His father had been forced to collect large sums of money in taxes which unpleasant task now fell to him. The people had suffered from the extortions of Crassus, while the high-handed methods of Antipas and now of Herod produced a state bordering on anarchy. The Parthians in the meantime had inflicted a defeat on the Roman legions and were advancing into Asia Minor. Mark Antony was away paying homage to Cleopatra.

When Pompey sent the disgruntled Aristobulus a prisoner to Rome he was building up a hostility that now bore fruit, for his son, Antigonus, having escaped from captivity, was now in contact with the Parthians, part of whose army had been detached to support him and was marching into Judaea.

Antigonus, after a short engagement at Drymus, entered Jerusalem.

In the city those Jews who were hostile to Herod laid siege to his palace and in the desultory fighting were beaten off. The prisoners were put in the temple area with a guard over them in the surrounding houses, but a counter-attack soon released them and their guard was killed. Inconclusive fighting continued for days. At the time of Penticost, when crowds massed into the city from the surrounding countryside, Herod, leaving a small guard at the palace, succeeded in restoring authority. At this point Antigonus suggested that the Parthian prince, Pacorus, should arbitrate. By this subterfuge the Parthians with five hundred cavalry were treacherously admitted into Jerusalem. Once in, they seized Herod's brother, Philail, with whom the arrangements had been made and executed him. Hyrcanus they also took, but accorded him more lenient treatment. In his place they put Antigonus on the throne.

Herod, now virtually friendless and without a following, was forced to flee the country. The flight was pathetic, gone was all the pomp and glory and never was the spirit of this haughy despot so nearly broken. He first took refuge in the almost inaccessible fortress of Masada by the Dead Sea, but was forced to fly from there to Petra where he was no more secure. He finally managed to cross the Mediterranean and, exhausted, to lay his grievances before his patrons Mark Antony, now back from Egypt, and Octavian (Augustus).

In Rome he entered the Senate to plead his cause and that of the youthful and legitimate heir, the Asmonean prince, Aristobulus, brother of his wife, Mariamne. The throne belonged by right to him in the absence of Hyrcanus whose release seemed most improbable and who might for all they knew have suffered the same fate as Philail.

So strange can the turn of fortune be that, instead of the crusts of patronage he had hoped for, he received more than he ever dreamed of. First, Antony made him tetrarch and then, with the assent of Octavian, he was able to persuade the Senate to declare him King of the Jews. It was, therefore, as a king that Herod returned, not alone, but with a force of Roman soldiers which Antony had put at his disposal.

He landed at Ptolemais where he added to his army additional Roman soldiers, many men of his own race and some foreign mercenaries. His military objective and political aim was to take Jerusalem; but first in order to ensure that his rear would not be threatened he marched on Joppa, which city quickly fell to him. He next proceeded to Masada to rescue those of his family and friends who he had had to abandon when he fled to Rome.

By now Herod's army had grown considerably, the Jews rallying in large numbers wherever he went. From Samaria, which was loyal to him, he ordered large supplies of corn, oil, wine and cattle to be sent to the area of Jericho for both his Roman and local troops. Antigonus attempted to ambush this supply column near Jericho, but Herod, anticipating this, had sent ten cohorts, five of which were Roman and five Jewish, plus a force of mercenaries, to protect the column. Antigonus's men were routed, the stores were distributed among the soldiers and a garrison was placed in Jericho. After this and as winter was drawing on the Roman soliders were sent into winter quarters in Galilee, Judaea and in Samaria.

Herod in the meantime with his Jewish troops and auxiliaries marched to Sepphoris which lay a few miles to the north of Nazareth and was at the time snow-bound. He took the place without difficulty, and then rounded up a large body of local Galilean bandits.

He now felt free to deal with Jerusalem to which he proceeded to lay siege, and after two years of resistance the city yielded to him. His triumphal entry took place on the twenty-fifth anniversary of Pompey's entry into the temple. On this occasion the great city was spared the horrors generally attending capitulation. Herod now displayed the nobler side to his character, saying that the dominion of the whole world could not compensate him for the suffering or death of one of his subjects. In fact, out of his own personal fortune, he actually bought the Roman soldiers off their rapacious and indeed legitimate looting.

No longer worried by problems in Judaea Herod was now prepared to assist his patron Antony in his fatal war at Actium. In the fortuitous and fickle way in which fate sometimes works he was restrained from this action, which might indeed have caused his downfall, by the machinations of Cleopatra. As a result he found himself embroiled in a war with the Arabs in the rocky and inhospitable country beyond Philadelphia. Though at first he suffered a set-back, when he returned later he was able to force the Arabs to battle in which he destroyed their fortress and annihilated their army.

Herod, with some justification, felt that with Antony's defeat at Actium, his own position might be in jeopardy. He, therefore, went to Rhodes there to put his case before Octavian who surprisingly said he had done no wrong and, in fact, took the opportunity to confirm him in his kingship, this time by decree. The diadem was placed on his head and those parts of his territories that Antony had conferred on Cleopatra were returned to him. Herod received a personal bodyguard of four hundred Galatians who had previously been assigned to the Egyptian queen.

Now secure in his possessions Herod was free to build the temples and palaces for which he was so famed. He had been strong enough to resist Cleopatra's amorous advances; he had retained Antony's friendship; he had been able to work harmoniously with Octavian; and he had shown himself to be an able politician, a shrewd commander and a loyal husband. In religious matters he was respected and in his public life he scrupulously observed the Law. All would have been well but for a strange streak in his character. Perhaps due to his Edomite extraction; perhaps to some twist of moral cowardice; or perhaps due to the intrigues of his sister, Salome he fell prey to attacks of insane jealously and of melancholy despair that drove him to do things for which he is loathed.

The death of Antigonus showed something of his callousness. On the capture of Jerusalem, Antigonus was, of course, taken prisoner and he threw himself on the mercy of the Roman, Socius, who knew no mercy. He had the luckless man lashed to a stake like any common criminal, scourged with rods and then ruthlessly beheaded. All through this pitiful and degrading scene Herod looked on and, although he cannot be considered as personally responsible for it, he nevertheless connived. Not surprisingly the horror of the outrage left a deep impression in the minds of the people.

Herod had married Mariamne and so, in theory at least, his house and that of the Asmoneans should have been united. Instead of bringing the blessings that it was fondly hoped would follow this union, it was destined to mark the beginning of a terrible and violent period in this man's life. Incredibly his first victim was Aristobulus whom he had befriended and whose cause he had so unselfishly pleaded in Rome. The boy, for he was still only seventeen years of age, assumed the office of High Priest in the absence of Hyrcanus. His fine stature set off by the gorgeous attire vividly recalled to all who saw him, the picture of his grandfather. The feelings of affection the people obviously had for the young Asmonean determined Herod to get rid of a potential rival. With a cunning hard to credit he had the boy drowned in an apparent accident at a party he himself gave in the groves at Jericho. When the corpse was brought to the surface and laid out on the marble floor Herod, as he looked at the face of his beloved wife's brother, still retaining its youthful bloom, wept bitterly.

Herod's battles were no longer against foes, but against himself. Jealously drove him on, stimulated by his own fears and the venom of his sister. Hyrcanus was the next victim. This unfortunate man, having returned from Babylon at Herod's invitation, who had promised to restore to him all those privileges that had been his before, was now ailing in health and old. By Herod's order he was tried, judged and executed on a trumped-up charge of plotting. Mariamne was his next victim and after that her two children, whom he loved, he had strangled.

Departed were the king's phantom fears of the Asmoneans; no member of this great family now stood in his way. But, departed also was happiness and gone was health His last agonizing moments were spent in foiling his sons by his first wife who were plotting his death. He died a despot, wracked by some foul disease.

Though Herod's pro-Roman instincts were equivocal, as was his attitude to paganism, of themselves they did not lose him prestige among his people. His main worries were caused by the Jewish resentment at the high scale of Roman taxation but, as long as he lived, there was no talk of insurrection and through him the Jews were content to swear loyalty to Caesar. On his death differences of opinion concerning his successor decided Augustus to divide the country into procuratorships, each procurator representing Caesar. Thus the people lost a king and protector in place of whom they got a magistrate and tax collector.

Whereas Herod had successfully acted as a link between the people and Rome, the procutators were a source of ever increasing irritation. It was, therefore, not surprising that discontent grew. To the antipathy between Jew and Roman there was added a mistrust, amounting to hatred, by the Hebrews for those Syrians who lived in the Hellenistic and Romanized cities.

Matters were not made any easier when the unpopular procurator, Cumanus, was replaced by one, Antonius Felix, of whom it was said he was like a king with the mind of a mouse. His high-handed severity reached a climax in a quarrel that broke out between the Jews and the Syrians in Caesarea. This is of interest to this story as it was at the investigation which took place in Rome that a Jew, Josephus, played an important part.

Josephus was the son of a priestly family of high standing and his mother, so he claimed, was of Asmonean extraction. He was a student of the law and before he became a Pharisee had studied the precepts of the Saducees and the Essenes. He had lived in the desert for three years with a hermit, Barus. As a Jew he was strictly orthodox. In politics he was pro-Roman, as his first name, Flavius, which he later assumed shows. He claimed that his addiction to Rome was a matter of policy and not of cult. The hard facts are that after having fought for the Jews he defected when it suited him and, after the fall of Jerusalem, he became a Roman citizen.

The Roman influences had their origins in his visit to the capital at the time when he went to plead the cause of two priests whom Felix had arrested. While there he made friends with a Jewish actor, a friend of Nero, and through him made the acquaintance of the emperor. Nero's Rome was dissolute; but the young Jew, knowing only the hills of Judaea found it wonderful, representing civilization and, above all power. This made him see his country in what he thought was its true perspective and, on his return, he tried without success to convert his countrymen to his view. Perspective, however, depends so much on which end of the telescope one is using, and the zealots in Judaea, face to face with the realities of oppression, knew which end they were looking through. Josephus was, nevertheless, caught up in the general revolt and his problem, which he really never satisfactorily solved, was to decide where his loyalties ultimately lay.

He showed to his best when sent to Galilee to organize the Jews in that difficult and important district. He first imposed a code of discipline and, emulating the Romans, he organized the men into tens, hundreds and thousands, each with its appropriate commander. He increased the number of officers and appointed subalterns so that soldiers should have someone to command them and someone to whom they could go when in trouble. He taught them the use of signals and the necessity for obedience to them. He stressed the importance of physical fitness and paid attention to morale training. He organized all towns and villages for defence, strengthening their walls and building these were they did not exist. He fortified the caves near the Sea of Galilee.

His dual achievement was that he prepared Galilee for the test that was to come, and, when it did and Vespasian invested Jotapaka, he commanded with skill and consumate bravery. His conduct on its eventual fall and his defection to the Roman camp make sour reading. After Jerusalem capitulated he became a Roman citizen and went to live in Rome where he wrote the 'Wars of the Jews.' To his credit he makes no attempt to whitewash or excuse his own actions and, as an historian, Josephus appears on the whole to be quite reliable.

The 'War of the Jews' started as civil unrest, the underlying causes of which were many. First, there was general resentment at high taxation; second, the unsympathetic attitude of many of the Roman procurators; third, the ill-disciplined actions of some of the Roman soldiery which culminated in outrageous conduct at the temple; fourth, the discord that existed between the Jews and those Syrians who occupied cities like Caesarea; finally, the activities of organized gangs of robbers who pillaged both Romans and Hebrews alike. The country was in fact in a state of general lawlessness in which even the Jews were not united.

The situation got so out of hand that the Roman governor of Syria was forced to intervene with troops. That he was unable to deal effectively with what were really not much more than civil disorder is remarkable but this was, as we shall see, due to his own ineffectiveness and to the inability of the Roman soldiery to deal with the situation.

This latter was remarkable, as the Romans had long since given up ideas of conquest and, from the days of Augustus onwards used their army only to hold what they had. Why was it that in Canaan they failed so lamentably to check civil disobedience from becoming all-out war?

Between the Euphrates and the Mediterranean Rome had six

legions, in all about thirty thousand men, or two divisions in modern parlance. These were highly trained and well armed. Each infantryman carried a long and a short sword in addition to a *pilum* or javelin. The latter was thrown at close quarters, and for in-fighting the legionary drew his sword. His body was protected by a breast plate, he had greaves on his legs and an ample buckler on his left arm. Each legion contained its own artillery which consisted of battering rams, catapults for discharging darts, and slings for hurling large rocks of up to sixty pounds in weight. The men were hard and fit. A legion could march twenty miles in the day over long distances.

Such an army was primarily suited for war; but, like many armies in peacetime, it often found itself employed on internal security and semi-police duties. In small numbers these well-disciplined troops could be of considerable consequence; in mass and in unsuitable terrain and circumstances they were vulnerable to guerilla tactics; their strength manifesting itself only when they were openly opposed by another army.

It was such a legion, the 12th, that marched into Canaan with Cestius, the governor of Syria, when he decided that the situation called for his intervention. Marching through Galilee where he found the towns deserted, he proceeded to Ptolemais and from there marched south to Joppa. Returning via Ceasarea and Lydda he advanced on Jerusalem. While he was moving up the defiles through Beth Horon he was attacked by Jewish guerillas who inflicted heavy casualties on his marching columns. When he reached Mount Scopus he halted for three days and on the fourth entered the suburbs of the city. Here he set fire to the houses. The Jews had, in the meantime, occupied the towers of the wall surrounding the temple which the Romans attacked without success over a period of five days. They next attempted to gain entry to the city from the northern wall by adopting the testudo method. On this the leading ranks placed their shields over their heads as they leant up against the wall as did the successive ranks in rear. Under cover of the testudo the miners started to undermine the wall. To the besieged this seemed to be the end. But, as so often happens in war, Cestius never realized how near to success he really was. Despairing of ever taking the place he ordered a withdrawal, as Josephus aptly put it, 'without any reason in the world.'

Cestius's retreat was as disastrous as it was inexcusable. In the approach to Jerusalem his troops had neither been deployed for nor prepared to meet the guerilla attacks to which they had been subjected. The hills on either flank were not piqueted nor were there adequate flank or rear guards. In his withdrawal the same lamentable errors were made. In addition his movements were slow and showed no awareness of the latent dangers.

After one day's rest on Mount Scopus, which gave the Jews time to lick their wounds and assess the situation, he moved down to his previous camp at Gabao only six miles distant. His unexpected retreat revived the courage of the defenders of Jerusalem, who now commenced to harry the rear of the retreating army, killing many Romans and capturing much baggage. Cestius stayed two days at Gabao during which time the Jews placed themselves on the high ground all around. Cestius now panicked and ordered the killing of all the animals carrying his baggage excepting only those on which his heavier weapons were transported. As the Romans passed through the defiles the enemy continued to attack them, holding off only when they were in the more open country. The Roman cavalry attempted to counter-attack but were defeated by the rocky and precipitous ground. The Roman infantry, immobilized by their own personal equipment, became targets for the Hebrew darts and by the time they reached Beth Horon their casualties had been immense. Only nightfall saved them from complete defeat. Selecting four hundred of his best men to act as rear-guard Cestius, under cover of darkness, fled with the remainder of his force. He was attacked on the flanks and in the rear, but the Jews wisely did not press their advantage when the Romans got into the more open country. The Roman rear-guard was surrounded and not a man escaped. Cestius lost all his artillery and baggage.

This was a serious blow. It came about because Roman tactics were wholly unsuited to the guerilla type of warfare and to the terrain. The heavily armed infantry, in the close hilly country through which they marched, were unable either to deploy or make use of their weapons. The cavalry, instead of being employed on the flanks, were pinned down in the valleys from which they could neither give warning of attack nor fight.

The Jews now set about organizing themselves for war. They divided the country into military districts in each of which they put suitable commanders.

In the meantime Nero had ordered his most experienced general, Vespasian, to assume command of all Roman forces in Syria. Vespasian's son, Titus, coming from Egypt, joined his father and brought two further legions with him. The whole force was augmented by large numbers of auxiliaries from Syria.

Titus joined his father at Ptolemais. When and not until he had inspected all his troops did Vespasian move. His order of march and arrangements for the protection of his column were as well thought out as those of Cestius had been futile.

First came his auxiliaries, who were lightly armed, and whose task was to search out the woods and look for ambushes. The main body of the advance-guard consisted of fully armed Roman soldiers. Next came Vespasian himself and his principal commanders. The commander was protected by a considerable body of infantry and cavalry. Then came the ensigns carrying the eagle. The main body followed with which was all the siege equipment and baggage. The rear was protected by a strong body of cavalry and infantry.

He marched east to the hills of Galilee and his route took him past the small town of Gadara from which the inhabitants had fled. In retribution for what had befallen Cestius he levelled the place to the ground. He then proceeded to Jotapaka, an important town which had already repulsed a Roman attack led by Placidus. The place had been prepared for defence by Josephus and he was now in fact in command.

It took the Romans forty-seven days to occupy the place and then it fell largely through the treachery of one man. That Jotapata was able to hold out as long as it did was owing to two factors; the offensive type of defensive tactics Josephus adopted and the natural strength of the position. In regard to the latter the principal advantage was that it stood on a rugged mountain and the slopes leading to the walls were steep and in places precipitous. Furthermore, the position had the advantage that it could not be overlooked from any side. The walls were high and they were strong and protected where necessary by deep ditches.

As the Romans approached the city the Jews went out to attack them but were beaten back and under a hail of arrows were forced to take shelter behind their walls. Vespasian attempted a direct assault which was beaten off by a spirited counter-attack in which the Roman losses though small had the effect of making them more cautious. The enemy now employed their siege equipment and started showering the defenders with missiles.

Under cover of this concentrated fire the Romans brought up heavy battering rams. When these seemed to be meeting with success the Jews protected their walls by letting down sacks which they had filled with chaff and, as the Roman soldiers came forward to remove these, they were met by a hail of darts. Vespasian next constructed stout hurdles under cover of which he built earthen walls or banks and on these he erected towers, from which his Arab archers were able to shower their darts on the defenders whose plight now was beginning to seem hopeless.

At moments when despair grips men's hearts the power to resist can reach great heights; so it was with the Jews at Jotapaka. As they fought on their courage grew and every little success buoyed them up to greater efforts. Mixing bitumen, pitch and brimstone with dried wood and setting fire to this mixture they soon had the banks and their towers transformed into a flaming inferno.

Nevertheless, the end was inevitable. Whereas the defenders could receive no reinforcement, the attackers were constantly helped by the arrival of fresh troops and so, as time wore on, the Romans by sheer numbers began to wear down Josephus's men. Tired by perpetual fighting, as they slept one night, they were betrayed by a man who led Titus's soldiers past the sleeping sentries into the city. Thus ended an epic defence.

Josephus with forty others escaped and hid; but realizing the hopelessness of their predicament, and at Josephus's personal instigation, they decided to draw lots, the basis of the idea being that the second to draw would kill the first and so on to the end. No one would thus fall into the Roman hands who, in any event, would kill all whom they captured. Josephus in the luck of the draw was the last. He did not keep the bargain and saved his life at the cost of his soul.

He defected and joined the Roman camp. Vespasian, who had heard much of this strange man, was anxious to meet him. A friendship undoubtedly grew up between the two and when, later, Vespasian went to Rome Josephus adopted his family name of Flavius.

Sweeping across Galilee the Romans moved over the Jordan to Gamala, a larger city than Jotapata and a stronger one too. It was situated on a rocky ridge on high ground overlooking the Sea of Galilee. It was rather like a camel in shape hence its name (*gamal*, that is 'camel'). In the rear where it abutted on to the mountain the approach was somewhat easier than elsewhere, but here the people had constructed a deep ditch. The houses were close together almost one on top of the other and making the place look as though it would fall down on itself. On the south flank was the citadal and above that was a precipice. It was served by spring water within its walls. Josephus had been responsible for the construction of its defensive walls in front of which were deep trenches. It had already withstood one siege and its inhabitants were confident of their ability to withstand another.

The taking of Gamala was remarkable since the Romans, having forced an entry into the city, were compelled to withdraw. Under cover of a shower of arrows and missiles Vespasian had managed to get his battering rams into position and with these succeeded in creating breaks through which his soldiers poured. In the labyrinth of streets that were steep, narrow and tortuous, the Jews fought every inch of the way.

The Romans were confused and their casualties heavy. Those who were in front were forced on by the pressure of those behind and many sought cover in the houses on either side. Some of the terraced houses commenced to collapse bringing down others with them. In the dust, the heat and the confusion losses were heavy. The defenders, hurling bricks and rocks and seizing the swords of the wounded and dead, turned confusion into rout. The general himself, who was in the higher parts of the city, was cut off and forced into a fighting withdrawal. He was fortunate to escape with his life.

The error had been over-confidence and impetuosity; and these, in a spirited address to his men, Vespasian warned them against. Incautiousness in battle and impetuosity were not, he said, Roman qualities. The city must be attacked again; this time, however, the progress must be a methodical advance from objective to objective.

In his next attempt Vespasian did not make use of battering rams, but relied on his miners. Three soldiers of the 12th Legion worked long and silently under the high tower and, when finally they removed five of the largest stones from the foundations, the tower collapsed. This time the Romans did not rush headlong through the gap; instead, Titus, with a picked band of horsemen and infantry, led the van, after which the attack progressed methodically from street to street until the complete capture of the city.

While this siege had been in progress a party of Roman cavalry numbering some six hundred, under the command of Placidus, moved up the Vale of Esdraelon to Mount Tabor where a considerable force of Jews had dug in. Placidus suggested they might parley and guaranteed their safety if they would agree. In fact he did not trust them and so, when they came armed and commenced to attack his comparatively small force, he was prepared. His strategem was somewhat similar to that of Joshua at Ai.

He feigned retreat and, when he had drawn the Jews well out into the open plain, he wheeled about and counter-attacked, killing many and cutting off the retreat of the remainder.

Deborah, on this same Mount Tabor, had until Sisera's chariots were immobilized by the mud, resisted the temptation to leave the strong position she held. Impetuous attacks may be indicative of great élan, but as in this case they can result in disaster.

Events outside Canaan now began to exercise their influence. A serious revolt broke out in Gaul and in the capital the affairs and the conduct of Nero were giving cause for offence. His tyranny and dissolute life had led the Senate to desert him in favour of Galba, the imperial governor of Eastern Spain (Hispania Tarraconensis). Nero fled to the villa of one of his ex-slaves and there he died.

On Nero's death civil war broke out and after the short reigns of Galba and Otho and in the confusion Vitellius seized the throne. A soldier, he had the support of the veteran legions of Gaul and Germany and the Guards in Rome. However, the legions of Egypt and Syria had already proclaimed Vespasian emperor, and these were joined by those of Moesia, Pannonia and Illyricum. Vespasian left Canaan and with Titus and part of his forces in that country marched to Alexandria, there to watch events. When his supporters under Antonius Primus invaded Italy from the north and, marching on the capital, defeated the forces of Vitellius, declaring Vespasian emperor, he left for Rome. Before departing he went into detail with his son, Titus, for the settlement of the revolt in Judaea.

At a time when moral standards were low and tyranny was rife, Vespasian stands out as a leader of impeccable character. Of him Tacitus said no one promoted simplicity more than he with his peculiar old-fashioned way of life. Though he was a stern disciplinarian he was liked by his troops. His slightly receding close-cropped hair, his large smiling mouth, his shrewd deep-set but kindly eyes gave him a benevolent look, while the breadth of his forehead indicated a capacity for thought and study worthy of one who was to wear the purple.

When his father had left Titus marched with his legions across the Sinai Desert to Gaza, which he reached in five stages averaging thirty miles a day over a dusty, hot and arid wilderness. To march six deep, as his men did, and for over ten hours a day was a feat indicating both fitness and fortitude. We have the details of this march and the places of halt from Josephus, and there seems no reason to doubt their accuracy.

The order of march followed that normally adopted by the Romans. In front went all the auxiliaries who acted as scouts and a screen for the main body. High up were the engineers for road making and laying out of the camps at each stage. Next in the column the commander marched with his personal bodyguard where he was well placed to make decisions for deployment or for battle as the circumstances should demand. Then came a large body of pikemen followed by the horse of the legion, after which were the artillery and engines of war. Between this and the main body of the army were the tribunes and heads of cohorts and the ensigns with the eagle. Behind the main body marched the baggage followed by a strong rear-guard of infantry and cavalry.

After a short rest at Gaza, Titus proceeded to Ceasarea via Askalon and Joppa. Here he had arranged to concentrate his army which he reviewed before moving, and he told them of his intention to capture Jerusalem, if necessary, by force.

In the Roman army command was personal. Legionaries would go anywhere with a man whom they saw, whom they knew, who could talk to them and who, above all, was valiant in battle. Titus fulfilled all these requirements. His decisions were reached only after he had consulted his commanders. This idea of a council of war, often ridiculed, had the advantage that all not only knew what they were going to do but why they were asked to do it; and it meant also that the commander had the advice and help of his capable subordinates before his decision was finally made. This practice Titus adopted during the more difficult stages of the siege of Jerusalem and on more than one occasion.

Cestius had, in his advance to and withdrawal from the city of Jerusalem, made the error of moving via the traditional routes following the valleys. Titus chose otherwise. Marching due east across the plain he got on to the central massif and thus put himself on commanding ground where his troops if required could deploy and where he would not be surprised.

Halting a few miles short of Jerusalem he went forward with a force of six hundred cavalry to carry out a personal reconnaissance. He wished to see the defences for himself and, more important, to discover whether he would meet with opposition and what form this might take. He was not left in doubt for long. He and his escort were ambushed and attacked in force, he himself only narrowly escaping death.

He had hoped then, as indeed he did right up to the end, that he would be able to take the city with a minimum of bloodshed and of destruction of its historical and holy buildings. In fact the siege turned out to be a long and bloody conflict in which the casualties on both sides were heavy and during which Jerusalem was destroyed.

I have already referred to the natural strength of this great walled city. Now, however, it was even more formidable. It was protected by three walls. The effect of the inner wall was to give depth to the defence and to make it difficult for the attacker to deploy his man and his engines of war. The third wall, which had been commenced by Agrippa, had been completed more recently by the inhabitants themselves. It was immensely strong, its base masonry consisting of great stones over thirty feet long and sixteen broad to undermine and remove which was a well-nigh impossible task. The wall was forty feet high with turrets and towers rising a further five and thirty feet respectively. There were cisterns for the catching and holding of water.

At this stage Titus had no apparent intention of siege operations, his plan was based on an assault on the walls from Mount Scopus and possibly from the direction of the Mount of Olives. To this end he moved two legions on to Scopus and a third, which approached from the direction of Jericho, he placed on the Mount of Olives overlooking the Kidron.

The Romans seemed strangely to have under-estimated the reactions of the Jews. While it was known that within their

ranks there was considerable disunity, the Romans failed to
realize that when threatened with imminent danger from outside the Jews would unite. Neither did the Romans seem to
have learned that the Jewish defence would be based on offensive tactics and not rely merely on static defensive measures.
Vespasian's siege of Jotapaka should have taught this.

It is, therefore, not surprising that the inhabitants of Jerusalem, seeing the enemy concentrating outside the walls of their
city, should forget their internecine quarrels and attack.
Streaming out of the gates they assaulted the nearest Roman
camp with surprising success. This forced Titus to order
certain moves to improve his position, which the Jews took to
be a withdrawal, and for this reason renewed their attacks, again
with success. In the hand to hand engagement Titus for a
second time had to fight to save his life.

The Romans, under cover of a protective screen, now commenced to level off the ground on the north side of the city.
Houses, gardens and orchards, trees and walls were either
demolished or cut down and hollows and ditches were filled in.

The Jews' next step was to entice the Roman soldiers to come
to close quarters. To achieve this they simulated quarrels
among themselves. Pretending to eject the dissidents among
their ranks they turned a large body of people out of the gates.
These, appealing for help, told the Romans that they could lead
them into the city. Titus suspected this, for only on the
previous day he had sent Josephus on an unsuccessful mission
appealing to the Jews to come to terms. His men, however,
were deceived and swarmed forward only to find they had been
trapped. When they were close under the walls and between the
towers the suppliants turned on them while from the towers on
either side darts were hurled down on their heads.

The operations against Jerusalem passed through two stages.
The first consisted in a series of assaults of a conventional nature
which, while meeting with a degree of success, failed to force
the Jews to surrender. The second phase took the form of a
seige with all the horrors of slow starvation, sickness and disease
inherent in this kind of business.

Titus's attacks followed the traditional pattern of constructing banks, erecting towers and using battering rams. Initially these were successful and in fifteen days he had gained possession of the northern wall. The battle for the second wall involved grim fighting in which the bravery of the Romans was matched by that of the Jews, neither gaining much over the other. Titus moved everywhere, encouraging where encouragement was required and helping where help was needed. He counselled his soldiers against taking unnecessary risks, for a Roman soldier alive was better than a Roman dead. Eventually, though he succeeded in breaching the second wall, his men were driven back. This came about because Titus would neither permit the levelling of the houses nor the destruction of the wall as he still hoped that by adopting a conciliatory attitude he could persaude the Jews to concede. He was anxious to do as little harm as possible to the sacred buildings and to the temple and he issued orders to his men to kill no more than was essential and to refrain from destruction. The Jews, however, were not prepared to give an inch for they were fighting not only for their lives but for all they held most dear. In the narrow streets and in the houses, in the alley ways and on the wall they fought and they attacked, even sallying out against the Roman reserves. In this hand to hand conflict, which went on for days the Romans eventually got the upper hand and regained what they had lost.

The problem now was how to break through the third wall. Space was confined, it was difficult to erect towers to cover the positioning of battering rams (which in any event were unlikely to break down the wall) and the deployment of an adequate number of men to do all this was impossible. Titus continued to hope that he could avoid further bloodshed, so he sent Josephus once again to call on the Jews to surrender. Josephus got little else than brick-bats and abuse. He claimed that it was the leaders who were against compromise and that, left to themselves, the people wanted peace. The way the bulk of the Jews were now fighting and continued to fight seemed to belie this.

Titus now held a council of war. Was he to continue the

assault and throw in the whole weight of everything he had? There was no certainty of success here, and there was indeed a limit to the number of men that could be deployed, and he would have very heavy casualties. Alternatively, he could attempt so to seal off the city that neither food nor reinforcement could enter; but the total circumference of Jerusalem was over four miles and to encircle such an area effectively would involve a wide dispersion of his forces, leaving him weak everywhere and strong nowhere. Thirdly, he could surround the city with his own wall. This he would be able to patrol while retaining adequate reserves and thus avoid undesirable dispersion. So Titus built a wall.

This opens the final stage of the tragedy, a siege with all its consequences. To construct their wall the Romans wanted timber and for this every tree for more than eight miles round was cut down. From now in all directions only bare desolation met the gaze. The once proud and beautiful Jerusalem was largely a stark war-scarred heap of ruins standing in an area that was more than a wilderness, it was a veritable desert.

The horrors of this siege were terrible indeed. Old and young had suffered alike, women and children were stricken with famine and disease. In the streets people died in their hundreds and the lanes were filled with their dead bodies. The smell was nauseating. Children wandered about like shadows, their bellies swollen from lack of food. Burying the dead became impossible and many who dug graves died themselves while at their work. There was a silence everywhere as deadly as night. Titus, when he saw the corpses that had been thrown over the wall and lay in the valley, putrefying in the pitiless sun, wept. The misery of the people daily became more and more intolerable, and yet they went on fighting. While outside the Romans had food and water, in Jerusalem there was lack of both.

Amid such horrors the final act was grimly fought out. The inner walls were breached and one by one the towers fell. As the Romans gained first the outer buildings of the temple and then the temple itself they set fire to everything; the cloisters, the great gates and the temple burned. Nothing remained save smoking timbers and stench. This was the desolation of desolation again.

This fall of Jerusalem marked the death of a nation; a people survived, but one without a home and with little civic corporate entity. The end this time was as inevitable as it was tragic. The last but one of the great battles of biblical history had been fought and lost.

Two characters stand in this, each different to the other, yet each representing something of his own race. Of Josephus I have written and of the factors that affected his conduct. With regard to Titus I have commented only on his conduct as a commander and on the decisions which he made. He was a successful general and later a Roman emperor, but what was he like? He was young at the time, only twenty-nine when he succeeded his father in command. Handsome in appearance he possessed all the attributes of a commander, brave in battle, firm in decision, strong in a personal discipline which he insisted on in others. He spoke fluent Greek, was an able musician and a poet. He was both kind and sympathetic to suffering. Though brought up in the hard school of war he hated death and always strove to gain his military objectives with as little loss of life as possible, which, in an age that was brutal, was indeed remarkable. He represented all that was best in Roman culture; that Josephus fell under his spell is, therefore, all the more understandable.

21 *The massacre of Masada*

Jerusalem had fallen and revolt in Judaea was virtually stamped out; yet, in spite of this, the spirit of all was not broken. The Sicarii, the most fanatic and delirous of all the Jewish patriots who had fought in the holy city, withdrew to the fortress of Masada. Here, under the leadership of Eliazer, they made their final stand. In a place so remote, in waterless terrain and of such natural strength, they could, with some justification, feel themselves secure, if not invincible.

It was John Maccabaeus who built the fort at Masada and it was to this stronghold that Herod fled. Later, eight years after his return from Rome, it was the magnificent view and the grand remoteness of the place that decided him to build an elaborate, terraced and gardened palace here for his beloved wife, Mariamne. Masada, in its isolated splendour, seemed to brood over the Dead Sea, the whole length of which could be seen from its walls.

There is nothing so sunken, so desolate or so apparently doomed as this salt lake. The streams that feed the Dead Sea flow through nitrous soil and are themselves fed by sulphurous springs and, as though to trap the salt they bring, there is no exit to the lake. The evaporation that keeps the water level down causes a thick haze which often is impenetrable to the human eye, and the columns of mist that rise form clouds which produce violent storms. The jagged and treeless slopes of the hills of Moab on one side and the mountains of Judaea on the other are typical of the barren nature of this spot. Starting with the destruction of Sodom and Gomorrah and ending with the tragedy of Masada biblical history seems only to underline its sadness.

The fortress of Masada was on an immense rock hewn out by nature from the mountain range of which it was an isolated promontory. As it jutted out pointing north-east it could not be ignored and was a challenge to all who passed by. It was a lonely spot in a barren land. It was unapproachable from any side except by a tortuous track on the west over the deep declivity separating it from the Judaean heights, a track which Josephus aptly named the 'Snake.'

To Flavius Silva, procurator of Judaea, with his veteran tenth legion, fell the task of subduing Masada. The awful remoteness of the place was accentuated by the waterless wilderness of the Judaean uplands through which the Romans had to march. Across this they constructed a road for their army with its siege weapons, baggage, food and even water. Nowhere is one more forced to admire the Roman genius for engineering than in their achievements here and at the siege of Masada.

Silva's first steps were designed to cut off the garrison from supplies or reinforcement and to prevent their escape. To do this he adopted the plan of isolating the area with a siege wall. This he built to a height of about six feet with watch towers at regular intervals. Down the valleys and up over the hills ran this astounding wall, which, with the eight camps for his own troops, can be discerned today. The wall was under constant vigilance from the watch towers by day and moving patrols by night.

In order to get his battering rams up to the fort he had to construct an enormous ramp, nearly five hundred feet in height and over eight feet broad at the top, and the whole reinforced with great baulks of timber. It was a prodigious achievement, little less than that of building a pyramid. For the work he employed enforced Jewish labour which, in addition to his army, had to be watered and fed.

Towers were erected and the battering rams which eventually broke down the wall put in position. The defenders had, however, been busy and had constructed an inner wall of timber that they had packed with earth, which the blows of the battering rams only seemed to make this more compact. The Romans solved their new problem by setting the whole thing on fire; but the wind, changing direction, forced them to withdraw temporarily. Going back to their camp for the night they returned at daybreak with their scaling ladders. Climbing these with great shouts of enthusiasm they entered to conquer.

No soldier met them, none did they see, only smouldering embers from dying fires met their astonished gaze. Then quietly, across the open, two women with five small children clinging to their mother's garments came towards them. No one else was there, not a soul to be seen, for no one else was alive. The story these two women told was as macabre as it was possible to hear.

When Eliazer and his men realized that the die was cast they decided that not one of them should fall a prisoner and that they should leave not so much as one soul to become a Roman subject. Ten men were selected by lot to slay the rest. Every man, clasping his wife and his children in his arms, lay down on the ground and gave his neck to his executioners. At the end nine of the ten were killed by one. He, the last, after having seen that not a man was still alive, set fire to the place and ran his sword through his own body. These two women had hidden themselves with their children and were the sole survivors of a garrison that had been nearly one thousand strong.

The siege and massacre of Masada brings to an end the great battles of biblical history. Epic conflicts had been fought by and over the people of Canaan; sometimes the country had exercised an influence far beyond its confines. Sometimes the inhabitants had been merely pawns in a far larger political field; but, whatever their role, of wars they had experienced plenty. The military and political lessons of those ancient times are as applicable today as when they were enacted. Weapons, equipment, transport and methods of communication may differ, but the frailty and the strength of human nature remain unaltered.

Epilogue

The Canaan of biblical history is the Israel of today. It stands now as it stood in the past, apparently secure but precariously poised between the peoples on its flanks. Its vulnerability lies now as it did of old in its geographical position and its strength in its people.

As there were the seeds of trouble between the Hebrews and their neighbours, so now is there conflict between the Arabs and the Israelites. Wise statesmanship can bridge this gap and, whereas military strength can produce a strong military position as it did with David, only political wisdom can consolidate this state of affairs. Solomon did this as did the Asmoneans.

The more one studies the battles of biblical history the more convinced one becomes that the elements that make for military success or failure remain constant. Leadership is what people yearn for and when this is forthright the masses react. Joshua, David and Judas Maccabaeus showed this.

Terrible as war today can be, it was equally terrible in the past. Men, women and children suffered and great heroics stirred them to great sacrifices. They were stirred by the heroism of Jonathan at Michmash and by the bravery of Eleazar at Beth Sur. Under great strain and when persecuted, resistance movements have shown the true character of a people; that of the Maccabees was repeated in Europe when

Nazi tyranny enveloped France, the Low Countries and the Scandinavian peoples.

Although Canaan has reverted to its biblical name of Israel the clouds of war continue to hang over its pleasant hills, across Jordan and in the wilderness to the south; but if white-capped Mount Hermon looks down on a troubled land it is still a beautiful one, 'flowing with milk and honey.'

Glossary and gazetteer

ABILA. A Greek city situated twelve miles east of Gadara on a branch of the Yarmuk.

ABELMEHOLA. On bank of a small stream running into the Jordan from hills of Samaria some fifteen miles south of Gilboa. Abel generally used in conjunction with another word means 'meadow.'

ACCHO. Later Acre, and in Greek and Roman times Ptolemais. Port on northern promontory of bay bearing this name. Some six miles to north of Carmel.

ADULLAM. 'Cave' of, in the Shephelah some nine miles north of Hebron, an easily defended area with plentiful water supply. ('Cave' is really a mistranslation and should be 'fort.')

AI. East of Bethel, meaning 'a stone heap.' Abraham rested between Ai and Bethel.

AJLON. Vale of, sometimes called 'the valley of the smiths' and in Hebrew Ge-Naharashim. Its entrance is to the east of Lydda, and up to the Beth Horons and on to the Plateau of Gideon and Jerusalem.

AKRABBIN. The ascent or heights of, generally known as 'the scorpions.' It was a line of hills that overlooked the Vale of Salt at southern end of Dead Sea.

ALEXANDRIUM. Fortress of, sometimes called Sartabeh and Kurn Surtabeh. Played important part in wars of the Jews and Romans. Herod confined Mariamne in it and there buried her two sons whom he murdered. Precise position not identified beyond doubt, but is said to have been on spur of hills of Samaria running close down to Jordan where its position overlooking the road from Damascus to Jericho gave it strategic importance.

AMMON. A kingdom to east of Jordan bordering Moab in south and Giliad in north. Its capital Rabboth Ammon, later Philadelphia and the Amman of today.

ANTHERDON. On coast two and a half miles north of Gaza.

ANTIOCH. On the Orontes, built by Seleucus I and named after his father Antiochus. The disciples first called Christians at Antioch. As a capital city it vied with Alexandria; it epitomized Babylonian influences of cult and splendour.

APHEK. Important town on road from Vale of Jezreel to Damascus in hills of Golan to east of Sea of Galilee from which it was about four miles distant.

ARABA. The natural continuance of geological rift in which ran the Jordan and the Dead Sea. It stretched south to reach the Red Sea at Ezion Geber.

ARBANA. River, bursts in the Anti-Lebanon through narrow gorge from mouth of which it fanned out in seven streams, providing water on which Damascus depended.

ARBELA. (a) In Canaan on west shore of Galilee, famed for caves in which Herod hunted bandits. Used also as place of refuge at time of Judas Maccabeaeus; (b) Ancient town in the country between the Greater and lesser Zab on the Tigris. The battle Alexander fought here when he overthrew Darius in 331 was fought sixty miles away at Gaugamala.

ASHDOD. About midway between Joppa and Gaza. Important town in fertile Plain of Philistia and one of the five great cities of the Philistines, the others being Gaza, Askalon, Ekron and Gath.

ASHTHOROTH. Lay some twenty miles east of Sea of Galilee on tributary Yarmuk in the land of Bashan.

ASKALON. On coast twelve miles north of Gaza, name derived from shakai, to weigh or pay.

ATAROTH. In Moab, believed to have been one of the cities of Reubin.

AZEKAH. One of the fortresses of Judaea facing coast of Philistia. Strongly built with eight towers it lay in commanding position in Vale of Elah, near where David met Goliath. It, with Lachish, stood out against but eventually fell to Nebuchadrezzar.

BASHAN. Often known as 'The Bashans' lay north of Gilead and east of Jordan, bound on south by River Yarmuk and north by the Heights of Hermon.

BETHBESI. Unlocated.

BEERSHEBA. Sometimes called the Well of Seven, lay at foot of Judaean hills facing Negeb.

BETH AVEN. Wilderness of, the highlands lying immediately to east of Bethel.

BETHEL. On the Great Central Range between Shechem and Jerusalem.

BETH HORONS. On the easiest and most direct route to Jerusalem from the coastal plain. Lower Beth Horon at 1,240 feet covered the entrance to the hill country and Upper Beth Horon at 1,730 feet covered the Plateau of Gibeon and the road to Jerusalem.

BETH REHOB. Precise location uncertain, but believed to be near Dan.

BETH SHEAN. Sometimes spelt Beth Shan, in Greek times renamed Scythopolis. Its importance lay in its position commanding the entrance to Vale of Jezreel.

BETH SHITTAH. On lower and eastern slopes of hills across the Vale of Jezreel opposite Mount Gilboa.

BETH SUR. Strong fortress on road from Hebron to Jerusalem, at head of valley of the Sur, one of the principal roads leading to heart of Judaea from coastal plain.

BOSRA. A later city of the Decapolis some fifty miles due east of Scythopolis.

BYBLOS. Ancient Phoenician port to north of Sidon. It is from this name that the word bible is said to be derived.

CAESARAEA. Port built by Herod to serve Sabaste some twenty miles south of Carmel.

CAESARAEA PHILIPPI. Temple built of white marble by Herod at source of Jordan near Dan. Name altered by Agrippa to Neronas but reverted later.

CARCHEMISH. Battlefield on which Egyptians under Necho were routed. Lay on west bank of Euphrates, about two hundred and fifty miles east and a little north of Damascus.

CARMEL. There are two Carmels; (*a*) the mountain and associated range that terminates on the southern promontory of the Bay of Accho; (*b*) Carmel in Judaea, about seven miles south of Hebron.

COELE-SYRIA. The term used by Alexander to denote Canaan and Syria; it did not include Phoenicia.

DAMASCUS. Seventy miles inland from the Mediterranean, watered by the Abana. In terms of age it probably preceded Babylon and Memphis and as a great city outlived them both.

DAN. One of the streams that contest the honour of being the source of the Jordan. The mound from which the waters spring is called Tell el Kadi.

DECAPOLIS. The original ten cities were—Scythopolis, the only one west of Jordan, Pella, Gadara and Hippos on the road to Damascus, to the south-east were Dion on an undiscovered site south of Pella, Gerasa and Philadelphia and further east were Raphana on a tributary of the Yarmuk and well beyond was Kanatha, the most easterly of all. Finally the tenth was Damascus.

DOK. Fortress of in foothills four miles north-west of Jericho and believed to be of Philistine origin. It covered an important road to the heights of Ai and Bethel.

DOR. Ancient point of landing south of Carmel, originally belonging to the Thekel who came from Crete, was one of the most northerly possessions of the Philistines.

DOTHAN. Plain of, on the historic route from Egypt to Damascus. It ran eastwards from the Plain of Sharon opposite Aphek passing by Eingannim, the modern Jenin, before turning north to Esdraelon. It was here Joseph's bretheren cast him into a pit from whence he was rescued and taken to Egypt.

DRYMUS. Location uncertain.

EBAL. See SHECHEM.

EDOM. Later called Idumaea by the Greeks. The area between the Dead Sea, the Gulf of Akaba and the Sinai Peninsula, the present Negeb.

ELAH. Vale of. The word connotes large evergreens such as ilex. Opening on the coastal plain opposite Ashdod it was one of the important valleys through the Shephelah leading to the highlands of Judaea. Its important tributary, the Sur, ran south leading to the Plain of Mamre and the fortress of Beth Sur.

EMMAUS. On the foothills two miles to the south of the Vale of Ajlon and close to the town of that name.

EPHRAIM. The term Mount Ephraim covered the whole tableland of Samaria south of Gilboa. The best translation of mount in this case is 'the hill country of.'

ESDRAELON. Plain of, the great area stretching from the Jordan to the Mediterranean. It was bounded on the south by the feature of Gilboa and Carmel and on the north by the Hills of Galilee. It was sub-divided into the Vale of Jezreel in the east and the Plain of Accho in the west.

EZION GEBER. The topmost point of Gulf of Akaba and the port Solomon developed as a centre of industry as well as of shipping.

GABAO. Location uncertain, but probably near Gibeon on road to Beth Horon.

GADARA. (i) A hill to south of and overlooking the Yarmuk about five miles from Sea of Galilee. (ii) In his march from Ptolemais into Galilee Josephus refers to Gadars, probably Gabara, the first important village some eleven miles inland.

GAMALA. On the great road from Scythopolis to Damascus on a long camel's neck-like hill filling the middle of the gorge lay Gamala.

GALILEE. Meaning the Ring or Circle, originally called Galil ha Garin, or Ring or the Gentiles. Few Jews settled here after the return from Babylon, but they came back at the time of the Maccabees, and Galilee became properly Jewish under John Hyrcanus.

GATH. Sometimes called the City of the Giants. It is the generic name for 'winepress' and was applied to several villages, Gath Rimmon. No more is known of its precise whereabouts that that it lay inland on the borders of Israel, probably near Ekron.

GAZA. Has been called the counterpart of Damascus, a harbour from the wilderness and a market for the nomads. Lies today where it lay in the most ancient times.

GEZERIM, MOUNT. See SHECHEM.

GEZER or GAZAR. A bastion of the Shephelah opposite Ramleh, high, isolated and fertile.

GIBBERTHON. A Philistine fortress in the foothills some six miles north-east of Lydda.

GIBEON. Plateau of, a few flat miles north of Jerusalem, always been on the easiest route from the coastal plain to the capital.

GIHON. Spring of, on the east side of Jerusalem where the rock slopes to the Kidron lay the spring, the interpretation of which is the 'bubbler.'

GILBOA. Mount of, to the south of and overlooking the Vale of Jezreel, the descent is rocky and steep. In fact the Gilboa feature runs in a great crescent the southern end of which faces Pella across the Jordan and the northern drops to the well of Harod, a total distance of some eight miles. The western slopes are gentle.

GILEAD. The high territory east of Jordan between the Yarmuk and the Jabbok rivers.

GOMMORRAH. See SODOM and GOMORRAH.

HARAN. On the river Habor, a tributary of the upper Euphrates.

HAROD. Wells of, in the Vale of Jezreel at the north-east end of the heights of Gilboa.

HATTIN. Horns of, on a gentle rise on the barren plains of Galilee about five miles inland from the Sea of Galilee and north-east of Tiberias.

HAZOR. Within sight of the Waters of Moram, now called Lake Hulah.

HEBRON. Ancient city lay on a hill to the north-west of the present Hebron. It commanded the entrance to the highlands of Judaea and was a market place of great antiquity.

HERMON. Mount, sometimes called 'Mount of Bashan' and at others the 'Hermons,' the land of the Ituraean archers.

HEROSHETH. At the point where the Hills of Galilee meet the Carmel Range. It is the gateway between Esdraelon and the Plain of Accho.

HOR. Mount, uncertain but probably the Heights of Akrabbin overlooking the Vale of Salt; Turkish Mount Madera.

HORMAH. Probably part of the Akrabbin, but unlocated.

IDUMAEA. See EDOM.

IJON. On a promontory some five miles to the north of Dan. Near Halom where Joab defeated Shobach.

JABESH GILEAD. On the high ground on southern bank of the Jabbok about ten miles east of the Jordan.

JAHAZ. A strong point on the Arnon river in Moab, in the south-east corner of Gihon's territory.

JERICHO. Probably meaning 'fragrant,' five miles to the north of the Dead Sea, called a city of palm trees in stark contrast to the country over Jordan and the rugged hills of Judaea.

JEZREEL. Vale of, bounded on north by the Hills of Moreh and Galilee, on the south by Mount Gilboa where it widens into one of the broadest stretches of the Jordan valley. At Bethabara it drops into the river and here is the ford where tradition has it that John baptized Christ.

JOPPA. Called Jaffa by the Arabs, a port of great antiquity where timber from the Lebanon floated down the coast was shipped to Egypt.

JOTAPAKA. An important village in Galilee which Josephus fortified and defended against Vespasian. It was in a commanding position in the foothills on the direct road from Ptolemais to Galilee.

JUDAEA. In early biblical times called Judah. A barren and rocky tableland stretching from Bethel to Beersheba.

KADESH or KEDESH. On the Orontes about one hundred miles north of Hermon.

KIDRON. The Brook Kidron, a deep valley separating Jerusalem from the Mount of Olives.

KARIATHAIN. In central Moab ten miles to the east of the Dead Sea.

LYDDA or LOD. Was settled by the Jews after the exile. Famed as the place of martydom of St. George and for his tomb.

LACHISH. An important fortress in the southern Shephelah.

MAACAH. With Beth Rahob and Zobal small Aramaean states probably in the 'Hermones.'

MAHANAIM. Exact location not known, it was east of Jordan. It is presumed to have been north of the Jabbok and not far from Jordan.

MASADA. Fortress on the Judaean hills overlooking Dead Sea.

MEDIBA. Unlocated.

MEGIDDO. A strong fortress commanding the entrance to the Vale of Esdraelon from the Plain of Sharon across the Carmel Ridge.

MICHMASH. A fortress town on the road from Jericho to Ai and Bethel.

MIZPAH or MIZPEH. A strong position some 2,600 feet up and about four miles from Jerusalem.

MOAB. The barren and hilly country north of Edom and south of the Nahalial river beyond which lay Ammon.

MODIN. On the road to Jerusalem below Lower Beth Horon and about seven miles east of Lydda.

MOROM. The waters of, present Lake Hula.

MOREH. Hills of Schechem and the Vale of Jezreel.

NEBO. Mount, in Ammon twelve miles east of Jordan and opposite north extremity of Dead Sea.

NAZARETH. Overlooking centre of Plain of Esdraelon.

NEGEB. Translated 'south,' but literally meaning dry and naked land.

OLIVES, Mount of, on east side of the Kidron.

PANEAS. At the source of most eastern stream of Jordan at foot of Mount Hermon. Its beauty deservedly entitles it to be called 'the very sanctuary of waters.' It was here that Herod, hard by the shrine of Pan from which the name Paneas is derived, built Caesaraea-Philippi.

PARAN. Wilderness of or desert of loneliness. The present Negeb.

PELUSIUM. Ancient port of Egypt, now represented by two mounds close to coast twenty miles east of Port Said.

PHILADELPHIA. See AMMON, Amman of today.

PTOLEMAIS. See ACCHO.

RAMATHAIM. On the lower slopes of Mount Ephraim some eleven miles north-east of Lydda.

RAHOB. West of Dan between Jordan and Litany rivers.

REPHAIM, Vale of, see VALE OF SOREK.

RIBLAH. On the Orontes to the south of Kadesh.

SAMARIA. The district of, was bounded on the north by Esdraelon and the south by Judaea. It was by comparison a fair land which included the Gilboa range and the Mount Ephraim area. The city was originally built by Omri on a hill in the valley leading down from Shechem. The Assyrians called it Beth Kumri. When Augustus gave Samaria to Herod he renamed and enlarged it, calling it Sebaste, the Greek for Augusta.

SEBASTE. See above.

SALT, Valley of, the low lying valley at southern end of the Dead Sea.

SCOPUS, Mount, meaning 'Prospect,' on north side of Jerusalem.

SCYTHOPOLIS. On the site of Beth Shean. See the DECAPOLIS.

SEPPHORIS. Three miles to the north of Nazareth, in the lower Hills of Galilee.

SENEH. So called from the thorns upon it, lay on south side of the Michmash gorge.

SHARON. The maritime plain between Carmel and Joppa in Hebrew meaning 'level,' but in Greek and Roman times it was known as the 'forest.'

SHECHEM. In modern times, Nablus. The ancient town, six miles east of Samaria, lies on the watershed of the Hills of Samaria and is flanked on the north by Mount Ebal, the dominant feature of the district, and on the south by Sezerim only slightly lower.

SHEPHELAH. Range of foothills lying between the Plain of Philistia and the mountains of Judaea; it was the debatable ground between the Philistines and Israel and between the Maccabees and the Syrians. The names meant 'low.' It was cut by three important valleys—Ajlon, Sorek and Elah.

SHOCOTH. On the slopes south of the Vale of Elah.

SHUNEM. Four miles to the north of Jezreel.

SIDDIM, Vale of, where lay the cities of Sodom and Gomorrah, supposedly submerged in the waters of the Lower Dead Sea.

SIDON. Like Tyre was originally on an island. Of the two Sidon was perhaps the older. In the Old Testament and in Greek literature Phoenicians are often called 'Sidonians,' a name probably derived from that of the god Sid.

SODOM and GOMORRAH. See SIDDIM.

SOREK, Vale of, the ancient Vale of Rephaim one of the shortest and most important routes into Judaea.

SUR, Valley of, where Vale of Elath gets to the back of the Shephelah it turns south into the valley of the Sur, sometimes called the trench between the Shephelah and the mountains of Judaea. Near its head is the fortress of Beth Sur.

TABOR. A dominant feature in the Vale of Esdraelon to the east of Nazareth, a bare, isolated mountain which dominates eastern Esdraelon.

TIRZAH. Uncertain but probably a little to the north of Shecem, than which it was probably older.

TYRE. See SIDON, from which it lies about twenty-five miles to the south.

ZIKLAG. On the lower slopes of the mountains of Judaea some fifteen miles south-west of Hebron.

ZOBAH. with Beth-Rehob and Maacah unlocated.

Bibliography

Breasted, J. H., *History of Egypt*.
Encyclopaedia Britannica, 11th Edition.
Frazzel, S., *History of the Jews*.
Josephus, *The Jewish Wars*.
Keller, Dr. W., *The Bible in History*.
Palestine Exploration Fund Quarterlies.
Payton, L. B., *Early History of Syria and Palestine*.
Smith, G. A., *The Historical Geography of the Holy Land*.
Tacitus, *Annals of Imperial Rome*.
Yadin, Professor Yigael, *Masada, Herod's Fortress and the Zealots' Last Stand*.

Index

GENERAL SIR RICHARD GALE

General Sir Richard Gale is one of the most distinguished soldiers of our time. When war broke out in
1914 he was at first rejected by the army, but when
he retired in 1960 he was Deputy Supreme Allied
Commander, Europe, and his previous post was that
of Commander-in-Chief, Northern Army Group,
Allied Land Forces Europe and British Army of the
Rhine. As a young officer in the Machine Gun Corps
he had a gallant record on the Western Front. Perhaps his greatest achievement was to raise the 1st
Parachute Brigade, and then lead the famous 6th
Airborne Division to Normandy as the spearhead of
the D-Day invasion. Later he was Deputy Commander of the Allied Airborne Army which performed
so brilliantly on the road to Germany. Immediately
after the war he played an important role during the
troubled days in Palestine as commander of the 1st
Division.

His life is that of a complete soldier, who has seen war
from every level, as a fighting man, a staff officer, and
a senior commander. In this book his wide, practical
experience of modern war, his intimate knowledge of
the terrain of Palestine, and his deep study of history
come together.